THE
ADDICTION
WORKBOOK

Patrick Fanning & John T. O'Neill, L.C.D.C.

MJF BOOKS

NEW YORK

Published by MJF Books
Fine Communications
Two Lincoln Square
60 West 66th Street
New York, NY 10023

ISBN 1-56731-209-8
The Addiction Workbook
Copyright © 1996 by Patrick Fanning and John O'Neill

This edition published by arrangement with New Harbinger Publications, Inc.

Manufactured in the United States of America on acid-free paper

MJF Books and the MJF colophon are trademarks of Fine Creative Media, Inc.

10 9 8 7 6 5 4 3 2 1

For my family
Patrick Fanning

and for mine
John O'Neill

Contents

1

How To Use This Workbook

This workbook is for people who want to quit drinking alcohol, or stop using other drugs such as cocaine, marijuana, amphetamines, sedatives, and so on. It will help whether you have already quit, or are just starting to think about quitting.

If you are currently very sick, suicidal, suffering acute withdrawal symptoms, or injured, you need more immediate help than a book can provide. Right now, check the "Alcoholism" listing in the *Yellow Pages*. Call the local council on alcohol and drug dependence. Explain your situation, and ask for their recommendation. You can also call Alcoholics Anonymous, and they will send someone to help you through your crisis.

If you are worried about your alcohol or drug use, you're not alone. In the United States, one in ten adults has problems with alcohol. One in twenty-five has problems with illicit drugs. That's over fifteen million people.

No matter how desperate and hopeless you may feel at times, you can quit for good and still live a satisfying life. Millions of people have successfully quit alcohol and drugs. Most have done it on their own. Eighty percent of people who recover from drugs and alcohol do it without intervention by others, without twelve step programs, without checking into an inpatient program, and without medication. Many guide their recovery with books like this one.

Those who quit on their own do so for many reasons. More than half make a rational decision after weighing the pros and cons. Some quit out of respect or concern for loved ones. About a third quit without a clear decision point—they just string together increasingly long periods of abstinence.

Theory

Some people believe that alcohol and drug misuse is basically a moral failing. Many experts say it's a disease. Others stress the behavioral patterns by which you form bad habits. Still others believe addiction to be a largely spiritual problem. People recovering from drugs and alcohol disagree about the nature of a Higher Power, or the degree of personal responsibility, involved in their problems.

This book is eclectic. We don't subscribe to any single theory about the nature of addiction, human nature, or divinity. We tend to put faith in the most recent research that shows substance *dependence* to be a brain chemistry disorder, and substance *abuse* to be a behavioral, habit-based problem.

If you're not a researcher, theory isn't all that important. What's important is what works. This workbook is a collection of proven ideas, exercises, and techniques that have worked for millions of people.

Many books, people, and institutions can help you in your fight to get free of alcohol and drugs—friends, doctors, hospitals, counselors, AA, medications, support groups, and so on. Be willing to try anything available to you that sounds good. But beware of anyone who tells you that their way is the only way. There are many paths to recovery.

Your Individual Recovery Path

This workbook is organized to help you design and negotiate your unique, individual recovery path. That path will take you through most of the stages described below; how long it takes, and the exact sequence of events, are up to you.

- **Decide** whether you are suffering from impaired control over your use of alcohol or other drugs. The next chapter will provide clear guidelines for making this judgment.

- **Get ready to quit** by overcoming denial and ambivalence, and by lining up the treatment, help, and support you will need. This is covered in Chapters 3 and 4. Even if you have already quit, it's a good idea to do the exercises in these chapters, since material you develop here is the foundation for work in later chapters.

- **Quit,** using the guidelines in Chapter 5 to determine how you will handle detoxification and withdrawal.

- **Go on record** by telling important, trustworthy people in your life that you have decided to stop drinking or using. Tell them how you intend to get help, and that you need their support. Chapters 5 and 10 offer practice in the communication skills you'll need. Part of this important step will be choosing a recovery mentor—a friend you like and respect who has been down this same path.

- **Take responsibility.** Philosophically, the position is simple: you are not to blame for your disease, but you are responsible for your recovery. Responsibility demands action on many fronts. Chapter 6 covers taking care of your body with proper nutrition and exercise. Chapter 7 teaches you to relax without alcohol or drugs, Chapter 8 helps you regain access to your legitimate feelings, and express them appropriately. Chapter 9 focuses on such spiritual tasks as making an honest inventory of your strengths and weaknesses. Chapter 10 coaches you in sharing your inventory with another trusted person. Chapter 11 is about making amends for your past wrongdoings.

- **Stick with it** by practicing the everyday art of relapse prevention, as outlined in Chapter 12.

Do the Exercises

This book can save your life. But to get any real, lasting value from it, you have to do the exercises. That's why it's called a workbook. It's not an inspirational pamphlet that you can leave on your coffee table and absorb painlessly while you go about other business.

The exercises work if you work at them. The results you get will be commensurate with your effort. Some of the exercises in the later chapters are very challenging, such as conducting a fearless moral inventory, or making amends to those you have hurt. Carrying out these exercises will be among the most difficult and rewarding things you will ever do in your life.

Easier exercises come first, followed by more difficult ones. As you proceed one step at a time, you will gradually gain the experience, insight, persistence, patience, and courage you need to reach your goal. You may take a long time to work through all the pertinent exercises in this book. Allow yourself six months to a year to finish. If your life is busy or stressful, better allow two years for the inevitable distractions, setbacks, detours, and delays.

Other Problems

You may have other problems besides alcohol or drugs. Thirty-seven percent of people with substance abuse problems also suffer from low self-esteem, depression, anxiety, phobias, chronic anger, or some other emotional or mental problem. Many more also have an addictive relationship to nicotine, food, gambling, sex, work, and so on.

Your priority must be to get free of alcohol and other life-destroying drugs first. You can't work on other areas of your life when you are actively drinking or drugging. Get straight first, then turn your attention to your other problems.

2

Do You Have a Problem?

Has anybody ever told you that you drink or drug too much?

☐ Yes

☐ No

Do others have a different opinion about your drinking or drugging behavior than you do?

☐ Yes

☐ No

If you answered *Yes* to either question, you may very well have a problem. Others can usually see harmful alcohol or drug use before you do.

Do you yourself sometimes think that alcohol, cocaine, marijuana, pain pills, or some other drug is causing problems in your life?

☐ Yes

☐ No

A *Yes* here is even stronger evidence that you have a problem, and that it's time to take action. Since alcohol and drugs tend to make you ignore or minimize danger signs, the mere suspicion that you might have a problem means that a very real problem has probably existed for some time.

If you answered yes to any of these three questions, you should read on to explore in greater detail.

What Exactly Is Your Problem?

There are many names for problems with alcohol and other drugs: alcoholism, addiction, problem drinking, dipsomania, chemical dependency, drug abuse, substance dependence, and so on. Many terms and definitions have been proposed by medical doctors, psychologists, social workers, researchers, hospitals, insurance companies, the courts, and other interested parties.

Regardless of what you call your problem, you can safely assume that it's serious, and that you need to quit, if you demonstrate any one of these danger signs:

- You drink or drug too much or too often

- Your drinking or drug use feels out of control

- Your use has endangered your life, job, relationships, or freedom

- You've developed a tolerance for alcohol or your drug of choice

- You have withdrawal symptoms when you stop using

The Crucial Difference Between Abuse and Dependence

Recent research shows that there are actually two distinct kinds of drug or alcohol problems: abuse and dependence. The crucial difference between them is whether you retain control over your drinking or drugging.

For example, George liked to party, especially on the weekends. From early Friday night to the wee hours of Sunday morning, he was on a tear. Monday mornings he often called in sick, or dragged in very late. His boss put him on probation. He was arrested for drunk driving one Saturday night, and lost his driver's license. His girlfriend moved out.

As bad as all this was, George's tolerance for alcohol remained about the same as it had been in high school—he didn't drink much more than he had in his earliest drinking years. He got a killer hangover every Monday morning; but, when it passed, he felt pretty good. He didn't get the shakes or the DTs, or need the hair of the dog the morning after.

George abused alcohol, but he did not develop the primary symptom of alcohol dependence—an inability to control his use. He had the *problem* of alcohol abuse, but not the *disease* of alcohol dependence. His drinking was a matter of choice and long habit, learned over the years; but he retained the ability to modify his drinking with willpower and reason. His path to recovery required him to make behavioral changes based on increased awareness, more accurate information, the lessons of adverse consequences, positive peer pressure, and just growing older and wiser.

On the other side of the coin, there was Jill, a part-time data processor and the devoted mother of two small children. Jill always showed up to work on time, kept a neat, clean house, and reliably picked her kids up at the day-care center every afternoon. Being a good mother was important to her, and she tried very hard to be patient, loving, and nurturing. She got along pretty well with her husband Frank.

Jill started smoking pot and drinking wine at night after the kids were in bed. At first this was just a way of relaxing. After a while, the one glass of wine with her husband became three or four, whether or not Frank had anything to drink. Instead of a toke or two, Jill usually finished off a whole joint.

When she noticed how much wine she was buying every week, Jill promised herself to cut down to two glasses a night. But more often than not she found herself unable to keep her promise. As things got worse, Jill tried to quit cold turkey, and was successful for a few days or even weeks at a time. Then she would convince herself that it was safe to start drinking again. Sometimes she was able to stick to her commitment and have only one or two drinks and half a joint. But before long, she would once again find herself losing control, sometimes passing out as a result. She still managed to get to work and the day-care center on time every day, and to be a good housekeeper and a conscientious mother.

Jill was suffering from the disease of chemical dependence—a pathological inability to control her intake of mood-altering chemicals. The give away symptom was her impaired control—she could no longer reliably predict the consequences when she took the first sip of her drink or drag on her joint.

Jill eventually found that it took more and more alcohol and marijuana to get the same results that small quantities used to produce. As her disease progressed, she found that without her nightly joint and glasses of wine, she felt agitated and anxious, and had trouble getting to sleep. As she lay in bed, her legs would twitch, and she felt hot and sweaty. Sometimes during the day, her hands shook.

Jill's increased tolerance and withdrawal symptoms showed that she was in the later stages of dependence on alcohol and marijuana. But she still managed to keep her house and family going. She didn't drive drunk, act noticeably odd in public, or endanger anybody. Nobody apart from her and her husband knew how much she drank and smoked.

Jill's disease of dependence was not as blatantly obvious as George's problem of abuse. Yet, unlike George, Jill couldn't correct her problem with willpower and reason. She couldn't "just say no," because her impaired control was not due to a lack of willpower, but was a matter of her biological affinity for alcohol and pot. Where George had the physiological capability to overcome his problem of abuse through choice and behavioral change, Jill needed outside help to overcome her disease of dependency. Her path to recovery involved medication that cut down her biochemical cravings, and a program of behavioral modification to help her avoid the first drink or drag.

Exercises

Complete the following two exercises to determine whether your problem is primarily substance abuse or substance dependence.

DSM-IV Substance Abuse Test

This test is based on the *Diagnostic and Statistical Manual, edition IV*, published by the American Psychiatric Association to guide psychiatrists and others in diagnosing mental and emotional problems. This questionnaire tests for the behavioral danger signs of substance abuse.

Answer the following questions quickly and honestly, without stopping to rationalize or split hairs. For each question, go with your first, most spontaneous response.

1. In the last 12 months, has using alcohol or other drugs occasionally caused you to miss work or school, perform poorly at work or school, neglect your children, or fail to perform household duties?

   ☐ Yes

   ☐ No

2. In the last 12 months, while under the influence of alcohol or some other drug, have you occasionally driven a car, operated dangerous machinery (such as a power mower), or participated in potentially hazardous sports (such as swimming or rock climbing)?

   ☐ Yes

   ☐ No

3. In the last 12 months, have you been arrested for driving while intoxicated, disorderly conduct, or any other substance-related offense?

   ☐ Yes

   ☐ No

4. In the last 12 months, have you continued drinking or using drugs despite fights or arguments with people close to you expressing concern about your drug or alcohol use?

   ☐ Yes

   ☐ No

If you answered *Yes* to one or more of these questions, you are abusing alcohol or drugs and need to make immediate changes.

When George took this test, he felt scared and cornered, because he saw himself in every item. He went straight to the Employee Assistance Program counselor at work, who spoke to him frankly and gave him some literature to take home. This dose of reality helped George realize the harm that alcohol and drugs were doing to his body, and he decided to change his lifestyle. Eventually, with a lot of determination on his part, and support from a few close friends, George found new activities to replace his partying, made new friends, and put his drinking and drugging years behind him for good.

When Jill took the test, she felt relieved. Apparently, curling up with her wine and weed each night hadn't gotten her into the kind of trouble that could officially be called substance abuse. But Jill wasn't off the hook.

DSM-IV Substance Dependence Test

Substance dependence, as opposed to abuse, doesn't necessarily involve extreme behavior problems. And yet dependence is more serious and life-threatening, because it acts like a progressive disease. If Jill continues her alcohol and pot use, she will eventually experience the array of pain and sorrow that characterize later stage alcohol and drug dependence.

Take this next test to look for the danger signs of chemical dependence. Answer the questions quickly and honestly. Don't give yourself time to rationalize—just give the first answer that comes to you off the top of your head.

1. In the last 12 months, have you been consuming more alcohol or drugs than you originally intended to at a given time, or does your drinking and drugging go on longer than you originally intended?

   ☐ Yes

   ☐ No

2. In the last 12 months, have you been wanting to cut down, or have you tried to stop or cut down, and not been able to?

   ☐ Yes

   ☐ No

3. In the last 12 months, has your tolerance increased—does it take more alcohol or drugs than it used to take to get you high, or achieve the desired effect? Or does a given amount have less effect than it used to?

   ☐ Yes

   ☐ No

4. In the last 12 months, have you had any withdrawal symptoms? For instance, have you felt shaky the morning after drinking, or thick-headed after smoking marijuana, or paranoid after using cocaine?

   ☐ Yes

   ☐ No

5. In the last 12 months, have you spent a significant amount of time procuring alcohol or drugs, using alcohol or drugs, or recovering from their effects?

   ☐ Yes

   ☐ No

6. In the last 12 months, have you been spending more time drinking or drugging and less time with friends and family, in work or school-related activities, or pursuing hobbies, sports, or other interests?

   ☐ Yes

   ☐ No

7. In the last 12 months, have you experienced any emotional or physical side effects—such as depression, anxiety, liver damage, or stomach trouble—but continued to use drugs or alcohol anyway?

☐ Yes

☐ No

If you answered *Yes* to three or more of these questions, you would be considered by a physician, psychiatrist, psychologist, social worker, or alcohol and drug counselor to be "substance dependent." Especially revealing are the first two questions regarding using more and more of your drug of choice, and not being able to cut down when you want to.

Jill flunked this test. Here is how she responded:

1. Greater quantity and duration than intended. Jill answered *Yes*, because, from the beginning, and on every subsequent occasion, she intended to just have a drink or two to relax.

2. Desire for change. Jill had tried to cut down several times and failed. Her *Yes* answer to this question was her main clue that she had a life-threatening problem. Social drinkers can quit or slow down anytime they want. Abusers, with a bit of encouragement and motivation, can do the same. Jill's inability to consistently control her use was what defined her unmistakably as substance dependent.

3. Tolerance. Although Jill hadn't noticed any increased tolerance for marijuana, she had noticed that it now took three glasses of wine to make her feel the way two glasses used to. So she answered *Yes* to this question.

4. Withdrawal. Jill hadn't been having the shakes or DTs. But she did have hangovers on many mornings, and she suspected that the pot was eroding her powers of concentration. Nonetheless, she gave herself a break and answered *No*.

5. Time spent acquiring, using, or recovering. Jill answered *Yes*. She didn't have to spend much time acquiring pot—a cousin of hers had her own plants, and was happy to sell to Jill. But she wasted two or three hours nearly every night drinking and smoking.

6. Less time for other people and activities. Jill had to admit that she used to spend more time seeing friends, taking dance classes, helping her kids with art projects, and playing the guitar. Her habit of drinking and drug use at night also made her reluctant to accept invitations from the parents of her children's friends to get together and socialize.

7. Emotional and physical side effects. Jill checked *No* on this one, but in all honesty to herself, had to say "not yet." Her husband pointed out that she was unhappy and worried about her substance use. "That's an emotional side effect right there," he said.

Denial Checklist

Whether you have decided that your problem is abuse, dependence, a little of each, or neither, you should do this exercise. It will give you a clearer picture of what you think and say to yourself about alcohol and other drugs. It will also remind you that you are not all unique or alone—the phrases in the denial checklist are things that millions of people have told themselves and others for hundreds of years.

There are many kinds of denial besides saying outright, "I don't have a problem." The exercise breaks denial down into categories: stonewalling, minimizing, blaming, excusing, rationalizing, distracting, and attacking. Check off any of the statements you have made to others, or thought to yourself. Add your own favorites. Take your time, over several days or weeks if necessary, to fully explore all the creative ways in which you deny chemical dependency or abuse.

Stonewalling

☐ I don't have a problem.

☐ I can handle it.

☐ I'm not hooked—I can quit any time I want.

☐ Leave me alone—it's my business.

☐ I'm not hurting anyone but myself.

☐ So what?

☐ (Other) _____

Minimizing

☐ Sure I drink (smoke, snort, etc.), but it's not a problem.

☐ It was just a little dent in the car. At least I didn't hit anyone.

☐ It's no big deal.

☐ At least I didn't behave as badly as _____ .

☐ I made it home all right. Everything must have been okay.

☐ It will be all right if I just apologize and cool it for a while.

☐ (Other) _____

Blaming

☐ It's not the booze (coke, pills, etc.), it's the stress (coffee, cigarettes, allergies, medication, etc.).

☐ It wasn't my fault—it was (_____'s) fault for getting me drunk.

☐ I need it because of my bad back (nerves, rotten childhood, etc.).

☐ My wife (husband, mom, kid, etc.) drives me to it.

☐ I would have been all right if I hadn't mixed drinks (drank on an empty stomach, been sold coke cut with speed, etc.).

☐ I need it to deal with _____ (a person or situation).

☐ (*Other*) _____

Excusing

☐ I'm self-medicating. It helps me relax (cope with pain, digest, etc.).

☐ It's been a day that would drive *anyone* to drink.

☐ I got carried away because I was so happy (sad, mad, upset, nervous, etc.).

☐ Everybody makes mistakes once in a while.

☐ I'll have just one drink (hit, etc.) to steady my nerves.

☐ I must be doing okay—I always get to work on time (manage to cook dinner, finish assignments, pick up the kids, etc.)

☐ I'm not hung over. I have a touch of flu (food poisoning, etc.).

☐ My mom and dad and all my aunts and uncles and cousins drink. It's practically a family tradition.

☐ I'm under an incredible amount of stress right now.

☐ We're Irish—what do you expect?

☐ (*Other*) _____

Rationalizing

☐ A nightcap will help me sleep; and, if I get a good night's sleep, I won't feel such a strong need to drink tomorrow.

☐ I need the hair of the dog that bit me.

☐ It's hot (cold, rainy, nice, etc.), let's have one.

☐ I'm already loaded. One more won't make any difference.

☐ I'll quit tomorrow.

☐ I deserve a reward.

☐ I need one for the road.

☐ As long as you're buying . . .

☐ I deserve to blow off steam once in a while.

☐ It's a social lubricant.

☐ Okay, I blew it this time. But I'll never do it again.

☐ Life is short. Live it up!

☐ I need a little lift when I'm down.

☐ Drink is my only friend.

☐ Let's celebrate.

☐ Many leaders, artists, and intellectuals were big drinkers or druggies. For instance, Churchill drank excessive amounts of brandy, Coleridge ate opium, and everyone knows about Edgar Allen Poe. Half the great poets in the world were falling-down drunks at one time or another in their lives.

☐ I broke my pledge and had one. I might as well have another.

☐ For Christ's sake, you have to toast the bride!

☐ I'm just a rebel.

☐ I like living on the edge.

☐ *(Other)* _____

Distracting

☐ Alcohol and drugs aren't the cause of my problems. They're just a symptom of my crazy life.

☐ I don't know why I have this strange pain *(when you know it's probably an ulcer or liver damage caused by alcohol . . .).*

☐ We need more fiber in our diet *(when you know your diarrhea and/or constipation are caused by drinking . . .).*

☐ My allergies are awful today *(when you have the coke sniffles . . .).*

☐ You'd drink too if you had my life. Let me tell you about . . .

☐ *(Other)* _____

Attacking

- ☐ You've got a lot of nerve talking about *my* drinking!

- ☐ Get off my back!

- ☐ As soon as I unwind a little, you're breathing down my neck.

- ☐ You're just like my mother—nag, nag, nag.

- ☐ I'll stop doping (drinking, smoking, etc.) when you stop throwing money away (get a job, stop crying all the time, stop cheating on me, etc.).

- ☐ Why don't you clean up this dump instead of counting my drinks?

- ☐ Oh yeah? And who wrecked the car (ran over his own dog, set the mattress on fire, etc.)?

- ☐ *(Other)* _____

Do any of these phrases sound familiar? Admitting to yourself that you have a problem with drugs or alcohol is very difficult. But it's the first step toward quitting for good, and reclaiming a better life.

When Jill went through the above exercise, she recognized many of her own ways of denying, excusing, and rationalizing her problem. It started her thinking about the many ways in which her family history and social isolation allowed her to keep drinking and smoking pot without having to fully count the costs or admit the toll it was taking on her health, relationships, and self-esteem.

When George completed the denial checklist, he had to confront his own rationalizations for over-the-edge behavior: "It's just wild oats," "I deserve to unwind," "I can stop any time I want," "I'm basically a party animal. Why not enjoy life while I'm young?"

Where Do You Go From Here?

What conclusion have you come to after working carefully through this chapter? Can you fill in these blanks?

I _____
                    (your name)

- ☐ *abuse* _____ .
                    (substance)

- ☐ *am dependent on* _____ .
                    (substance)

If you felt able to do so, congratulations on your courage in facing difficult truths about yourself. You can go on to the next chapter with confidence.

If your exploration of your problem has shown you to be significantly dependent on alcohol or other drugs, pay special attention to the section in Chapter 5 on new craving-blocking drugs. Also plan to spend extra time working on Chapters 6 and 7, so that you can optimize your physical health by improving your nutrition, getting plenty of exercise, and practicing regular relaxation.

If this chapter has shown you to have an abuse or habit-based problem, you may benefit from concentrating on Chapters 8 through 12—expressing feelings, exploring spirituality, improving communication skills, making amends, and preventing relapse by avoiding high-risk situations.

Perhaps you suspect that you are chemically dependent or that you tend to abuse drugs and alcohol; but you aren't 100 percent convinced. Or you're convinced, but you just can't bring yourself to write it down, or tell anyone about it right now. In that case, you can go on to the next chapter to see what's next. But, eventually, you will have to return to this section, and come to a definite conclusion about your use of drugs and alcohol. Remember that the ultimate question is, *"Can I consistently keep promises to myself about my use of alcohol or drugs?"*

If you've decided that you *can* keep promises to yourself, and don't have a problem, why are you still reading this book? Maybe you'd better take one more run through this chapter to make sure it doesn't apply to you.

This precaution goes for counselors, teachers, students, clergy, and concerned family members or friends who are reading this book to learn how to help somebody else. You can't effectively help others with substance abuse or dependence if you're denying substance problems of your own.

3

Getting Ready To Quit

Having admitted that you are dependent on, or tend to abuse, alcohol or other drugs, are you ready to quit?

That can be a frightening question. Quitting always involves a chance of failure, and may require major life changes. Neither are experiences that you would seek out in the best of times, much less when you are physically, emotionally, and spiritually damaged by a substance you both love and hate.

How do you know when you're ready to quit? Well, reading this book is a good sign. It means that change is on your mind. It means that you recognize that alcohol and drugs are a problem for you. This chapter will help you get ready to quit by developing a very clear picture of the pros and cons of quitting, and gathering the information and resources you will need to make quitting a reality.

Denial and Ambivalence

When you have a problem with drugs or alcohol, and you haven't quit yet, you'll hear the word "denial" bandied about by people who want you to cop to your problem and get well. Many assume that chemically dependent people are blind to the enormity and scope of their problem. Denial is often supposed to grow out of some character flaw, such as fear of conflict, false pride, stubbornness, inadequate willpower, or reluctance to face unpleasant facts. Many sober people talk about those with a drinking problem as being "in denial," as though they were totally blind to their condition and doomed until they somehow see the light.

However, the truth is that most people are not blind to their drug or alcohol problems. They may rationalize, create alibis and excuses for their behavior, repress unpleasant knowledge or memories, and even suffer blackouts that affect recall. But they are not completely in denial.

If you use too much alcohol or drugs, you are more likely to be ambivalent. You probably *can* see the damage that booze or cocaine causes. You *can* envision how many of your problems would be solved if you quit smoking pot or taking uppers.

But it isn't that simple, is it? Addiction issues are never black and white, but contain many areas of gray. You probably have some compelling reasons for continuing in your familiar patterns of substance use. You undoubtedly can see drawbacks to quitting.

For example, Richard was a microwave engineer for an aerospace company in Northern California. From his dad he had inherited the tradition of the Friday night martini hour, the Monday Night Football six-pack, and the anniversary bottle of Mumm's champagne. He added his own traditions—the Mimosa brunch on Sunday, the wine-tasting tour with visiting engineers, the margarita Mexican lunch, and the late-night brandy snifter while watching sexy movies with his girlfriend Lorraine. Alcohol was woven into the fabric of Richard's life. He used it for celebration, relaxation, social lubrication, consolation, and titillation.

Richard couldn't imagine life without drinking, even though he was aware of some of the costs of his drinking: his marriage of eight years had recently broken up, partly because his wife had quit drinking and he hadn't. Some days at work he was so hung over that he just stared at a circuit diagram, head propped up on his arms, dozing while trying to look like he was reading. Sometimes after heavy drinking, he woke up at three in the morning, depressed and scared and unable to go back to sleep for hours. He woke up one morning after a friend's birthday party not knowing how he had gotten home or even what happened after about ten o'clock the night before. He was getting fat and short of breath. He was afraid to go to the doctor for a checkup, fearing that he might find out he had the same kind of heart trouble that killed his dad.

The rational part of Richard's brain was beginning to acknowledge the price he was paying for his drinking. But another, more primitive part of his brain clung to his love affair with alcohol. It took Richard a long time to sort out the pros and cons of continued use.

To get a clearer picture of your own reasons for quitting or not quitting, spend the next few days completing a "decision box," explained below.

Decision Box

In the appropriate squares, write down both the good things and the bad things about quitting. Then write down the good things and the bad things about *not* quitting. When you're done, you'll have a complete picture of all the factors influencing your decision to quit.

	Quitting	Not Quitting
Good Things		
Bad Things		

To help you out, here are some checklists of good and bad things others have noted about quitting and not quitting. You should read through the lists slowly and carefully. They may introduce many considerations you haven't thought about yet. It's well worthwhile to make your decision box as broad and all-encompassing as possible, and to be as honest as possible. This kind of clear-minded assessment of consequences is a valuable skill to learn, one that you will need later—after you quit—for relapse prevention.

Good Things About Quitting

Physical Implications

☐ Better health in general

☐ Longer life

☐ Less chance for cirrhosis of the liver

☐ Lessened damage to pancreas and other organs

☐ Reduction of high blood pressure

☐ Prescribed medication can do its work without interference

☐ More energy

☐ May help you stop smoking as well

☐ Stronger voice—you can start singing again

☐ Weight reduction

☐ More attractive appearance

☐ You'll sleep better

☐ Improved digestion

☐ You'll be able to get back in shape

☐ *(Other)* _____

Mental Implications

☐ Greater sanity

☐ Better memory

☐ Better judgment

☐ Enhanced ability to focus your thoughts and actions

☐ Clearer mind for creative work

☐ You'll be able to get more done

☐ You'll free up the energy you've put to use conning yourself into believing that you don't have a problem with alcohol or drugs

☐ You'll worry less, have less anxiety and stress, and feel more relaxed

☐ You'll have more time for hobbies, community work, home improvement, and so on

☐ You'll be able to concentrate on problems other than your addiction

☐ *(Other)* _____

Social Implications

☐ Better chances for saving your existing marriage/relationship, or the chance to create a sober relationship with someone new

☐ Enhanced ability to make peace with parents, siblings

☐ Opportunity to make new, more positive friends

☐ You won't be so cross or inattentive with your children

☐ You'll be able to enjoy a wider range of activities

☐ You'll save money

☐ You'll avoid the embarrassment, expense, and penalties of legal problems connected to using, dealing, driving under the influence, and so on

☐ More time for family and friends

☐ Improved productivity at work

☐ Ability to take up your favorite sport again

☐ Opportunity to redeem your reputation as a sober, productive member of society

☐ Enhanced ability to plan for the future

☐ *(Other)* _____

Spiritual/Emotional Implications

☐ Feeling of pride in having the courage to quit

☐ Chance for true happiness

☐ More genuine emotional life (emotions aren't tied to highs and lows of alcohol and drugs)

☐ More freedom (no longer a slave to alcohol or drugs)

☐ More control over your life

☐ More self-confidence

☐ Reestablishment of spiritual connection to God, self, others

☐ Ability to pursue higher aspirations now that substance abuse is no longer a problem

☐ Greater feeling of maturity

☐ Opportunity to make amends toward people you've hurt through your drinking or drug use

☐ (Other) _____

Bad Things About Quitting

Physical Implications

☐ Withdrawal symptoms

☐ Cravings

☐ Missing the feeling of intoxication

☐ Diminished pleasure in smoking, eating certain foods

☐ Weight gain (for instance, from quitting speed)

☐ Sleep problems

☐ (Other) _____

Mental Implications

☐ Sudden inability to drown out self-doubt, regrets, guilt

☐ Boredom

☐ Possible loss of agility and ease in writing, talking, being funny

☐ End of excuses for not dealing with other problems

☐ (Other) _____

Social Implications

☐ End to congenial evenings in the bar

☐ Your drinking/drug friends will feel abandoned

☐ Endless free time to fill

☐ Increased bashfulness, shyness, sense of reserve

☐ Intensified loneliness

☐ Loss of wine-making, beer-brewing hobby

☐ Awkwardness and self-consciousness at parties

☐ Inability to entertain businesspeople in accustomed style

☐ Fear that intimacy may be impossible without the social lubricant of drinking/drugs

☐ Greater sexual inhibition

☐ *(Other)* _____

Spiritual/Emotional Implications

☐ Diminished fun, spontaneity, sense of adventure

☐ Loss of self-image as a misunderstood rebel

☐ Inability to blame alcohol/drugs anymore

☐ Need to take responsibility for your actions

☐ Chance of failure—as long as you don't really put yourself to the test, you can always imagine that you'll be able to quit

☐ Feelings of being deprived of the high/comfort/ease that came with your use

☐ Feel naked, vulnerable, unprotected

☐ *(Other)* _____

Good Things About Not Quitting

Physical Implications

☐ Substance use brings you relaxation and ease

☐ Substance use helps you fall asleep

☐ Your chronic pain is relieved or diminished by alcohol or drugs

☐ You like the taste

☐ Your substance use makes food, cigarettes taste better

☐ You just love to feel high

☐ Your use stops the morning shakes

☐ Drinking stops the trembling and hallucinations of DTs

☐ (*Other*) _____

Mental Implications

☐ Drinking/drug use helps you worry less

☐ Nothing bothers you when you're loaded

☐ Drinking/drug use keeps you from obsessing about your problems

☐ Drinking/drug use slows the hectic pace of life

☐ Drinking/drug use relieves boredom

☐ Drinking/drug use makes you feel more creative

☐ Look forward to it all day

☐ (*Other*) _____

Social Implications

☐ Getting high is the only thing you and _____ like to do together anymore

☐ Using makes you feel part of your social crowd

☐ You have more fun at parties when you're high

☐ Alcohol and/or drugs are great for celebrations

☐ Substance use is part of your lifestyle

☐ You have more and better sex when you use your substance of choice

☐ Getting high provides a comforting ritual every evening

☐ Alcohol and/or your drug of choice reduces your shyness

☐ Social drinking is necessary for your business dealings

☐ (*Other*) _____

Spiritual/Emotional Implications

☐ Alcohol/drug use takes the edge off your loneliness

☐ Alcohol/drug use relieves depression—at least initially

☐ Alcohol/drug use helps you forget painful memories

☐ Alcohol/drug use drowns out some of your feelings of guilt

☐ Alcohol/drug use makes you feel powerful, confident (when high)

☐ Alcohol/drug use puts you in a nostalgic, sentimental mood

☐ Alcohol/drug use allows you to express your anger

☐ Alcohol/drug use makes you feel grown up

☐ Alcohol/drug use gives you the courage to face life

☐ Alcohol/drug use comforts you when you fail or lose out

☐ Alcohol/drug use makes you feel more loving

Bad Things About Not Quitting

Physical Implications

If You Use Alcohol

☐ Liver disease

☐ Inflamed or cancerous pancreas

☐ Ulcers

☐ Cancer of esophagus, colon, rectum

☐ Bladder infections and bladder cancer

☐ Kidney failure

☐ Hypoglycemia (low blood sugar)

☐ Diabetes

☐ Convulsions

☐ Hallucinations

☐ Pneumonia, bronchitis

☐ Lung cancer

☐ High blood pressure

☐ Congestive heart failure

☐ Anemia

☐ Osteoporosis (lost bone mass)

☐ Gout

☐ Diarrhea/constipation

☐ Eye tics

☐ Vitamin deficiencies

☐ Brain damage

☐ Decreased lifespan

☐ Obesity, excessive weight

☐ Fetal alcohol syndrome (in offspring of women who drink during pregnancy)

☐ Premature aging

☐ Impotence

☐ Irregular periods, infertility, inability to achieve orgasm

☐ Loss of the sense of taste and/or smell

☐ Increased chance of miscarriage, birth defects

☐ Hangovers

☐ Chronic weariness

☐ Sleep disturbances

☐ Morning shakes

☐ Eating disorders (alcohol replaces food)

☐ Interactions with prescription medications

☐ Offensive body/mouth odors

☐ (*Other*) _____

If You Use Marijuana

☐ Impaired short-term memory

☐ Heart disease

☐ Increased risk of lung problems—emphysema, cancer

☐ Weakened immune system

☐ Possible long-term brain damage

☐ Reduced sperm count

☐ Irregular menstrual periods

☐ (*Other*) _____

If You Use Cocaine

☐ Central nervous system damage

☐ Increased risk of heart attack

☐ Increased chance of stroke

☐ Risk of respiratory system collapse

☐ Aggravated high blood pressure

☐ Chronic sinus problems

☐ Inability to sleep

☐ Weakened immune system

☐ (*Other*) _____

Mental Implications (For Alcohol and Drug Use)

☐ Memory loss

☐ Blackouts

☐ Poor judgment—tendency to take unreasonable risks

☐ Feelings of stress, tension, anxiety, guilt

☐ Confusion—inability to focus or concentrate

☐ Arrogance

☐ Paranoia

☐ Tendency to behave in ways in which you would never allow yourself to behave when sober or straight (i.e., picking fights, forcing your sexual attentions on someone, shouting insults)

☐ (*Other*) _____

Social Implications (For Alcohol and Drug Use)

☐ Destruction of treasured relationships

☐ Trouble with the law

☐ Isolation resulting from antisocial behavior

☐ Limited options

☐ Setting the worst possible example for your kids

☐ Undermining family unity

☐ Devastating physical and legal consequences of drunk driving

☐ Possibility of hurting someone when drunk or stoned

☐ Problems with the law associated with buying or selling drugs and/or driving under the influence

☐ Loss of respect

☐ Financial difficulties resulting from loss of job, legal expenses, or costs of a drug habit

☐ Impaired ability to get or keep a job

☐ (*Other*) _____

Spiritual/Emotional Implications (For Alcohol and Drug Use)

☐ Feeling of being spiritually empty—that life is pointless

☐ Loneliness, isolation resulting from depression

☐ Poor self-esteem

☐ Feeling dependent on alcohol or drugs

☐ Guilt associated with loss of control—feeling like a disappointment to others

☐ Out-of-control anger

☐ Chronic lying about drinking and/or drug use

☐ Embarrassment

☐ Feelings of enslavement to alcohol and/or drugs

☐ Sense of regret about time and opportunities wasted

☐ Abject dependency on others to take care of you when you're drunk

☐ Paranoia and anxiety caused by cocaine

☐ Sense that everything is out of control

☐ Feelings of failure

☐ Excessive emotionality that gets in the way of daily functioning

☐ Apathy, passivity, sense of helplessness and hopelessness

☐ Depression

☐ Suicidal thoughts

☐ (*Other*) _____

Add It Up

Look at your Decision Box as a whole. Which squares have the most items in them? Which factors seem most important to you?

Rank the items in each square. Put a 1 by the most compelling item in each square. Put a 2 by the next most important item, then a 3, and so on, until you have ranked the top five considerations in each square.

Here are some of the entries from Richard's Decision Box, shortened and simplified for the sake of brevity. We include the number rankings Richard assigned to the five most compelling factors in each category.

Keep working on your decision box for several days, even weeks, if necessary. Add to it every time you think of another advantage or drawback to quitting or not quitting. Ponder each item, and change your rankings as your thoughts change.

Do the good things about quitting outweigh the bad things about quitting? Do the bad things about continuing to drink or drug outweigh the good things about continuing?

This is a calculation that only you can make: the elements of the equation are different for everyone. When you resolve all the pros and cons in your unique self-portrait of behavior and desire, does one path emerge as more inviting than the other? Do you feel drawn toward either one alternative or the other? Which is the path you'd like to see yourself on tomorrow, or next year, or even ten years from now? Which way will you go?

Write your top five good things about quitting on a 3x5 card. On the back of the card, write down your top five bad things about not quitting. Carry the card around in your shirt

	Quitting	Not Quitting
Good Things	Mind more alert Better health (1) Lose weight Get back in shape Ex-wife might relax visitation rules (3) Better at job (5) Sleep all night Self-respect (4) More energy to make other changes in my life (2)	There are many drinking traditions I enjoy (1) Drinking is part of my lifestyle (3) Drinking makes me feel sexier (4) It's just easier not to change (2) If I don't quit, there's no risk of failure (5)
Bad Things	Nothing to do at parties (4) Need whole new lifestyle (1) Can't visit wine country (5) Lorraine will dump me (2) Don't want to be part of the sanctimonious "recovering alcoholic" group at work (3)	I suspect I might have heart trouble (1) Shortness of breath Fat Hangovers My work suffers (5) Worry about driving drunk (2) Shorter life Night sweats Depression (3) Panic attacks Blackouts (4)

pocket, wallet, or purse. Take it out and think about it several times a day. Talk it over with a trusted friend who does not have a problem with alcohol or drugs.

The ranking numbers on Richard's Decision Box above show the point he arrived at after three weeks of reflection about his drinking. He realized that he was really worried about his heart, and afraid of dying at 60 of a heart attack like his dad. Quitting would improve his health in general, and his chances of warding off heart trouble in particular. He also realized how totally stuck he was in his familiar, comfortable lifestyle, which revolved around drinking. He thought back to things he had planned to do with his life, and had to admit that alcohol had killed his initiative, drive, and imagination. To say that his career was stalled was putting it kindly—his honest assessment was that he was already slipping in his boss's estimation, and that he might be facing demotion or layoff. Quitting alcohol would give him back some of his self-respect, and a sober lifestyle might impress his ex-wife enough so that she'd let him see his daughter more often. Some old wounds might begin to heal.

Special Considerations

You might ask why the only two options in the Decision Box are quitting or not quitting. Why isn't there space for "cutting down" or "tapering off" or "drying out for a while"?

These are common "warm turkey" methods, often tried instead of going "cold turkey" and quitting completely right away.

You might sample sobriety for a while, then go back to drinking or drugging. You might try tapering down, or a trial period of moderation for a while. Any move *toward* abstinence you can make at this point will be a positive step toward quitting in the long term.

But if you're chemically dependent on alcohol or drugs, you will eventually have to make a decision—and get the help and support you need to enforce it—to quit for good. It's been proven over and over again that moderation doesn't work nearly as well as total abstinence for the chemically dependent person. Remember that the criterion for dependence is impaired control—so "controlled" drinking will never work for you if you're chemically dependent.

If your problem is simple substance abuse, without a trace of chemical dependency, you may have some success with a program of moderation rather than total abstinence. But even for substance abusers, abstinence is usually easier and better than moderation, which demands that you make decisions about the extent of your drinking or drug use every single day, through all the ups and downs, parties and holidays, triumphs and disappointments, moments of strength and moments of need, for the rest of your life.

4

Finding the Right Help

First, the emergency procedure: If you are seriously ill, overdosed, or injured, get to an emergency care center now. Be sure to report as accurately as possible what amounts and types of alcohol and/or drugs you've been consuming. Emergency medical people are there to help, not to judge. Tell them the truth, and they'll be able to help you through the crisis.

If you are suicidal, chronically ill, or have acute withdrawal symptoms, you need more than reading material. You need to call for help right away. If you are unable to do so yourself, ask a friend or relative to check under "Alcoholism" in the *Yellow Pages* and call for you.

The first place to call is the local council on alcohol and drug dependency. Explain your circumstances and ask for a recommendation. Based on your need and ability to pay, staff members can suggest appropriate help options for you. You can also call the Alcoholics Anonymous answering service, often the nearest and most readily available source of help. If you request assistance they will send a volunteer member or two out to help you through your crisis. There are no strings attached—when you call AA, you are not joining or agreeing to participate in the program and there is no cost.

Yellow Pages Exercise

Even if you are not in an emergency situation right now, get out your phone book, and turn to the *Yellow Pages*. Write down some of the local phone numbers you find under "Alcoholism" and "Drug Abuse." This is a useful exercise for acquainting yourself with the resources in your community, and you'll have the information handy if you need it later on.

Right now, call at least the AA or NA number, even if you don't think you want to ask for help or attend a meeting. Get the places and times of meetings near you, and write these down on your phone list. The information will be there for you if you decide to use it later.

National Council on Alcoholism and Drug Dependence (800) NCA-CALL _____

Alcoholics Anonymous _____

     Meeting place _____ time _____

     Meeting place _____ time _____

Council on Addiction _____

Narcotics Anonymous _____

     Meeting place _____ time _____

     Meeting place _____ time _____

Women for Sobriety _____

_____

Other local hotlines or treatment programs _____

_____

_____

_____

_____

_____

_____

James is an example of how such a list can work for you. James went out drinking Friday night, hardly got any sleep, and spent all Saturday and Sunday watching football and drinking beer. He woke up on Monday with a terrific hangover, and called in sick with the "flu." Late that afternoon, he noticed how nervous he was: his hands were shaking, his stomach was churning, and he felt on the verge of doing something violent. He fantasized about going to his ex-wife's house and throwing a brick through one of her windows. Then he remembered that his daughter lived there, too, and James was overcome with a sense of shame and panic.

It was at that point that James decided that alcohol had finally gotten the best of him. Checking his list, he called a local number for the "Council on Addiction" in his area. When the volunteer answered, James said he'd like help "for a friend" who had a drinking problem. Such hotlines get lots of calls about "friends."

The volunteer, who was trained in crisis intervention, gave James the names of nearby treatment programs, as well as the times and places of local AA meetings. After a couple of false starts, James dialed AA, and found the volunteer to be understanding and personable. She only asked for James' first name, spoke to him nonjudgmentally, and found out whether he'd like someone from AA to contact him.

By then, James was shaking so badly that he was willing to talk to anybody who might be able to help or reassure him. Shortly after he hung up, a man named Tony called him, and arranged to get together at a local coffee shop. Tony shared enough of his personal story so that James knew at once that he was in the right company. A recovering alcoholic himself, Tony was honest, understanding, and kind.

Realizing that James might be suffering acute withdrawal—he was getting really shaky, and kept saying that he wished he had a drink—Tony offered to take James to an emergency care center that was headed by a physician who was himself a recovering alcoholic. This was James' introduction to the network of people in his community who were highly motivated by their own recovery to help newcomers.

The sympathetic M.D. gave James a shot of *Librium* to contain his withdrawal symptoms while his body detoxified itself from alcohol poisoning. Tony drove James home, and arranged to pick him up the following afternoon to attend an AA meeting.

James' shakiness had settled down by then, he thought about how a lot of his preconceptions about quitting and AA had been really inaccurate. He'd expected a lot of sanctimonious lecturing, but Tony's attitude had been friendly and helpful. James realized that there were people out there who understood his problem, and would be willing to help him, once he made the decision to reach out.

Doing It On Your Own

If there's no emergency, how about quitting on your own, without help? Perhaps you feel convinced that you've had enough of the melodramas and predicaments that drinking or drugging bring to your life. You're ready to quit, and you're sure you can do it, if you just make up your mind.

Well, maybe. Those who successfully recover from addictions have obviously found a way that works for them. In that sense, they "do it on their own." But any such plan usually includes a healthy portion of outside help.

To decide what kind of help or support you need, you first have to see your situation clearly. If you've been managing your feelings, relationships, and behaviors with alcohol or other drugs for a very long time, it's unlikely that honest self-appraisal is your strong suit. You should be suspicious of any inclination you have to tough it out alone.

The champions in the recovery game are those who can look honestly at their assets and liabilities, know what tools are available within themselves, but also recognize at what junctures they will need outside help.

To get beyond addiction usually means you'll have to tap into outside resources—even if you're a fiercely independent person who hates the idea of needing anyone else's help. In this one arena of your life—alcohol and drug use—you may be powerless to go it alone. For many people, this can be an extremely difficult reality to face.

Powerlessness

"Powerlessness" is a word that sparks an emotional reaction in people. It's clear that you are not completely without power. You have probably accomplished much in your life. The insinuation that you are powerless over mood-altering chemicals might be offensive.

However, it has probably been your inability to consistently keep promises to yourself about your use of alcohol and drugs that has led you to this workbook. Apparently the strong will, fine mind, and demonstrated discipline that may have characterized most of your life don't function as readily when it comes to drinking and drugs. Short of being forcibly locked up and deprived of your substance, you won't be able to quit until you face up to the fact that you have a problem, and will probably need some help solving it.

Consider Janie, who had a history of self-discipline and high achievement. She graduated near the top of her class at school, and went on to command a high salary and professional respect. During the running craze of the '70s, she quit smoking cigarettes cold turkey and started running. Her disciplined approach to the sport enabled her to complete two marathons. Her marriage was successful and stable, producing two children who were happy and well-adjusted.

Janie had never failed at anything she seriously attempted. So it was difficult for her to believe that she couldn't manage her intake of wine and vodka. Nonetheless, she tried unsuccessfully on numerous occasions to cut back or quit drinking. She could control it, or even stop, for a while. But, eventually, she always found herself unable to consistently keep promises to herself about her drinking.

It was a dismaying experience for Janie to have to ask for help—to admit that she was powerless to go it alone in this one narrow area of her life. Overcoming her addiction to alcohol finally involved getting help from other recovering alcoholics, her family, her friends, her doctor, and her therapist.

Janie found it useful and logical to conceptualize her powerlessness in the face of addiction as a brain chemistry disease. Mainstream science and medicine have proven that all drugs of euphoria operate in the pleasure pathway of the brain, the "medial forebrain bundle." This pathway passes through the area of the brain where instinctual survival drives—such as thirst, hunger, and sexual urges—reside.

Janie was fascinated to learn that some people are innately sensitive to the effect of alcohol and drugs. Researchers believe that this sensitization translates into an instinctive need, much like thirst or hunger. Once such a condition develops, the need for a drink or a drug is no longer a case of take it or leave it. Rather, you experience a deep, primitive drive towards chemically induced euphoria, originating at a level in the brain where willpower, reason, and good intentions simply don't operate. For Janie, this knowledge was of great help in accepting her essential powerlessness to stop drinking on her own.

Imagine that you are talking to a skid-row alcoholic. You ask him why he is still drinking, when it is obvious that alcohol has ruined his life.

"I dunno," he says.

"Is it because of the high you get?"

"Nah, I don't get any pleasure from booze no more."

"Then why do you drink?" you ask in wonderment.

"I dunno. I just have to drink." He can't explain his need for the alcohol, because the need occurs at a subrational level.

For down-and-out drunks, powerlessness has become pathological. Janie was still able to recognize her powerlessness and do something about it. What about you?

What Helps and for Whom?

Among the many kinds of self-help, support groups, treatment models, medications, and therapies, some work better than others. Respected research also demonstrates that some of these approaches are more effective for some kinds of people than others. Certain approaches don't help, and can even do harm.

A sensible starting point in building your personal plan for recovery is to make an inventory of the resources available to you. Books, magazine articles, counselors, and other people in the recovery movement can help you assess the relative effectiveness of these programs for a person in your situation, with your particular health profile, religious/cultural background, history of attempts at quitting, and type of addiction. It's also useful to look at how others who've been successful pursued the task of planning their own recovery efforts. Let's begin by describing the various organizations, disciplines, and programs that are among your options.

Alcoholics Anonymous (AA)

This daddy rabbit of the self-help movement was founded in 1935, and is embodied in the book *Alcoholics Anonymous.* The only requirement for membership in AA is a desire to stop drinking. The goal of members is lifetime abstinence, "one day at a time."

In simple terms, the program is based on twelve steps that involve accepting your powerlessness over alcohol, turning your life over to a power greater than yourself, making amends to those you have harmed, making a lifelong practice of these principles, and expending major efforts to help others who are still suffering from addiction. The founders of AA derived these principles from a composite of what religion, psychiatry, and medicine knew at the time about overcoming alcoholism. And yet, the steps have proved remarkably resilient over the years in the face of scientific experimentation, new discoveries in medicine and psychiatry, and the experiences of millions of recovering alcoholics. It has been said, "The world would be a better place if everybody practiced the 12 steps."

Because of its longevity and tradition of anonymity, AA often suffers from inaccurate stereotyping. Many people picture an AA meeting as a collection of red-nosed, middle-aged males sitting around in a smoke-filled room invoking God's help to avoid the next drink. A more accurate view of AA today would show a group of 25- to 35-year-olds, one-third of them women, in a nonsmoking meeting, sharing their experiences with a newer member who is worrying about how to stay sober during an upcoming round of business-related holiday parties.

Meetings vary widely in format, and are usually led by a volunteer, temporary chairperson. There are women's groups, gay groups, adolescent groups, agnostic groups, newcomers' meetings, Viet Nam veterans' groups, and so on. A typical, medium-sized city in the United States will have several hundred meetings a month.

Literature is available at modest cost from:

General Service Office of Alcoholics Anonymous
475 Riverside Drive
New York, NY 10115
(212) 870-3400

Facts To Consider

- It's been around for over 50 years

- There are 51,000 autonomous groups worldwide

- It began with two guys, now has 1.5 million active members, yet has never made any effort at publicity

- Empirical evidence shows that it has helped many people to stop drinking for good

- It's available almost everywhere in the world

- It's free

To honestly evaluate AA for yourself, you need to sample several different groups. It's fine to just show up on your own and check out a meeting. You don't need a special invitation. You don't need to have a particular belief or attitude, beyond the desire to quit drinking. No one will try to get you to sign on the dotted line, or commit to coming back to a particular group. Because each regular meeting develops its own unique character, you may have to try ten different meetings before you find the one where you feel most comfortable.

The one caution about AA is that members can sometimes get stuck in an unhealthy dependence on AA itself, to the exclusion of family, friends, or wider interests. Well-rounded AA members advise you to "keep going, but keep growing."

Narcotics Anonymous (NA)

Narcotics Anonymous (NA) was founded in 1953. Like AA, it takes the position that addictions are a disease characterized by powerlessness over drugs. Its program is based on the 12 steps, but the focus is on drugs other than alcohol.

NA literature asserts that "we are not responsible for our disease, but we are responsible for our recovery." Meetings closely resemble AA. Literature is available at modest cost from:

Narcotics Anonymous World Service Office, Inc.
Box 9999
Van Nuys, CA 91409
(818) 780-3951

Facts To Consider

- It's been around over 40 years

- There are 4,000 autonomous groups worldwide

- There are an estimated 150,000 members

- There's a lot of empirical evidence that it works

- It's free

As with AA meetings, different groups are composed of different types of members, and meeting styles may differ from group to group. You need to try several meetings of different groups to find the one that suits you best.

Rational Recovery

Rational Recovery was developed in 1986 by social worker Jack Trimpey as a nonspiritual alternative to AA. The approach is based on Albert Ellis's Rational Emotive Therapy. The program suggests overcoming your "beast brain" through a cognitive therapy technique called Addictive Voice Recognition Therapy (AVRT). AVRT theorizes that the addicted person can override the lower brain's voice of addiction by use of reason, and more powerful messages from the higher brain.

Like AA, Rational Recovery aims at lifetime abstinence for its members; and the only requirement for membership is a desire to quit. The steps to recovery do not include an admission of powerlessness or reliance on a higher power. Groups are usually led by trained coordinators. RR offers counsel, seminars, classes, hospital services, extensive literature, video and audiotapes, and newsletters for dues and fees.

Rational Recovery Systems, Inc.
Box 8000
Lotus, CA 95651
(916) 621-2667

Facts To Consider

- Compared to AA and NA, Rational Recovery is the new kid on the recovery block, and has not yet developed much of a track record.

- Offers a more truly "rational" approach than agnostic AA groups

- The technique will cost you more than AA group attendance, as materials are fairly expensive.

- The authors would not recommend this approach if developing humility is one of your recovery objectives.

Founder Jack Trimpey has little good to say about AA and other support groups, and suggests his program can replace conventional treatment. Consequently, even his kindest critics observe that Trimpey overstates the case for RR and undervalues more traditional alternatives.

Women for Sobriety

This organization was founded in 1976 by Jean Kirkpatrick, Ph.D. Her "New Life Program" aims to help women achieve sobriety through self-discovery. The program stresses learning new competencies, independence, self reliance, and emotional and spiritual growth.

The only requirement for women who want to join is a desire to stop drinking and change their lives. Members of Women for Sobriety often attend AA meetings as well. Small groups of six to ten women are led by moderators certified by the organization. The goal is lifelong abstinence. Women for Sobriety emphasizes a woman's emerging role and her need for self-esteem and self-discovery.

Literature is available from:

Women for Sobriety, Inc.
Box 618
Quakertown, PA 18951-0618
(215) 536-8026

Facts To Consider

- Much research suggests that women in recovery have needs and issues that are different from those of men.

- The program seems well-tuned to contemporary issues faced by women

- The general outlook of Women for Sobriety is very positive, hopeful, and supportive

Treatment Programs

Structured treatment programs for alcohol and drug dependence have undergone great changes as health-care budgets and restrictions have tightened. The once-ubiquitous Minnesota Model of 28-day in-patient care is no longer available under most health plans. Hybrid combinations of in-patient and out-patient approaches are far more common today.

The National Institute on Alcohol Abuse and Alcoholism (NIAAA) has initiated a well-designed and controlled study called Project Match to determine what kind of treatment works best for which kind of drinker.

Project Match studied three basic forms of treatment: Twelve-Step Facilitation, Cognitive Behavioral Coping Skills Therapy, and Motivational Enhancement Therapy. One thousand, seven hundred people with drinking problems were randomly placed in these three kinds of programs, each delivered over a twelve week period in out-patient settings.

Earlier treatment matching studies suggest that certain types of treatment do work better for specific kinds of clients. As this book goes to press in the Spring of 1996, final Project Match results are not available. You will no doubt read about the findings in the lay press.

Meanwhile, one of the best ways to find a good treatment program is to attend twelve step or other support group meetings, and ask around. Be careful—the person you're talking to might work for the program he or she is boosting. After a bit of investigating, you will hear about the programs in your area that have the best track record. You may also learn about programs to avoid.

Medications for Treating Addiction

Because of the rapidly growing body of knowledge about the neurochemistry of addiction, more and more medications for the treatment of addiction are being developed. At present there are more than a dozen medications undergoing trials for their efficacy in aiding recovery from alcoholism and drug addiction.

So far, only one drug, *Revia*™, has been approved for use by the Federal Drug Administration (FDA). *Revia*™ has been proven to reduce cravings and prevent relapse in abstinent alcoholics and heroin addicts. It is safe, nonaddictive, and has very few side effects. The data on *Revia*™ were so compelling that the normally conservative FDA streamlined their approval process for use of the drug for treatment of alcohol addiction.

Revia™ is neither a cure nor a magic bullet. For example, it does nothing to directly attack the neurochemistry of impaired control over alcohol use. But it does reduce cravings and prevent relapse, and thus is a valuable new adjunct to conventional treatment. The manufacturer, DuPont Merck, has developed a free support program as an additional aid to those taking the drug. For more information, call 1-800-4PHARMA; the operator can refer you to participating physicians or facilities in your region.

Nontraditional Aids to Recovery

Many alternative approaches to the treatment of addiction have been tried, and many— such as hypnotism, extreme diets, mega-vitamins, aversion therapy, and various approaches to controlled drinking—have been shown to be ineffective.

However, there are two nontraditional treatments that have recently shown unusual promise: acupuncture and alpha-theta brainwave training.

Acupuncture advocates can quote few controlled studies, but the limited research that has been done supports claims that the technique derived from Chinese traditional medicine can reduce craving, and lessen the severity of withdrawal symptoms, for both heroin and alcohol addiction.

Alpha-theta brainwave training operates on the theory that brain chemistry is out of whack in people with chemical dependency. There is some scientific evidence of diminished alpha and theta brainwave activity in such individuals. Using biofeedback techniques, clients are trained to adjust their own brainwaves into healthier patterns. The clinicians using this technique—which is also used for other disorders attributed to brainwave abnormalities, such as Attention Deficit Disorder—are making impressive claims. Studies conducted in 1990 at the University of Southern Colorado measured personality differences and changes among alcoholics who received alpha-theta brainwave treatment. The results showed increases in stability, abstract thinking, conscientiousness, boldness, imaginativeness, and self-control compared to a control group receiving traditional treatment. The technique is noninvasive, has no side effects, and is gathering a growing number of supporters.

Choosing the Right Treatment for You

An old backwoods hunter once said in response to a young braggart, "Show me your coonskins!" Good advice for someone investigating addiction treatment. Ask for proof of success. Talk to those who have tried these various programs. It's a buyer's market. We suggest attending a number of different support group meetings until you meet people like yourself who recovered successfully. Listen to these winners and take advantage of their wisdom and experience.

Your Personal Support Network

Your own network of personal support can be a more important element in your recovery than all the alcoholism experts, organizations, and institutions in the world. Your immediate family, relatives, friends, and acquaintances will have a profound effect on your efforts to get free of alcohol and drugs. The next step in lining up the right help is to systematically categorize everyone you know in terms of the role they're likely to play in your recovery.

Address Book Exercise

Go through your address book, computer files, phone list, Christmas list, datebook, revolving file, or whatever you use to keep track of people you know. Write down the names of everyone you contact or see frequently, dividing them into *Supporters, Neutral parties,* or *Underminers.*

Supporters	Neutral Parties	Underminers
_____	_____	_____
_____	_____	_____
_____	_____	_____
_____	_____	_____
_____	_____	_____
_____	_____	_____
_____	_____	_____
_____	_____	_____
_____	_____	_____
_____	_____	_____
_____	_____	_____
_____	_____	_____
_____	_____	_____
_____	_____	_____
_____	_____	_____
_____	_____	_____
_____	_____	_____

Don't forget to include your spouse and other immediate family members, or other friends or relatives whose numbers you know by heart. Don't forget people you hang out with at work, school, clubs, bars—people you wouldn't necessarily call, but with whom you're in regular contact.

Supporters are people to whom you'd be able to say, "I quit all my drinking and drugging for good," and expect to get the response, "That's great! I'm glad to hear it. What can I do to help?" These are the people with whom you want to spend a lot of your time.

Neutral parties are people who won't particularly care about your drinking or your abstinence, either way. They are not particularly good sources of support, but aren't in themselves sources of temptation. You can tell them about quitting or not, as seems appropriate to you in each case.

Underminers are people who may be chemically dependent themselves. They are still drinking and drugging, and would prefer you to keep doing the same. These are the people who will undermine your sobriety. They are the ones who will respond in some belittling or jocular fashion to the news of your quitting. "Oh, God—now it's going to be you, me, and your higher power. There goes all our fun!" Or, "What makes you think you have to quit? You can just go easy on it for a while. There's no need to stop cold turkey. You'll screw up your system!" Or, "Haven't you read about the latest research? A few drinks a day are *good* for you! Come on, let's pop this new Zinfandel I bought last week!" Or, "Ah, you're not so bad. Have a beer."

The best way to handle underminers is to avoid them. Don't invite them over. Don't go to their parties. If your spouse is an underminer, get into counseling together, or ask your spouse to go to Alanon. The same goes for any person you love but recognize as a negative influence in your mission to stay sober. Tell him or her, "I love you dearly, but the only way I'll agree to see you until you stop drinking/drugging, too, is at a twelve-step meeting. Quitting for good is even more important to me than our relationship—which will give you a good idea about just how important it is." Show no mercy toward those relatives and so-called friends who simply refuse to honor your need for their support. For some people married to underminers, this has meant separation and even divorce. For others, such a stand has been the beginning of reconciliation. For many others, it has meant rejecting old cronies and finding a whole new set of friends.

For example, Marcy quit drinking in April. For her birthday in June, her old friends Gail and Didi wanted to take her to lunch at La Plume, one of their favorite restaurants and watering holes. Marcy had to tell Gail, "Thanks, but I'm staying away from places like the Plume, places where I used to drink. I'd rather go to the Swedish bakery place. Or maybe we could go on a picnic—without any alcohol." Gail and Didi who were both heavy drinkers, told Marcy she was being a bore. Next thing they new, they told her, she'd be giving up sex or finding God. Didi said, "What's the sense in being alive if you can't celebrate with a nice bottle of wine on your birthday?" Marcy thanked them for their invitation, and firmly turned it down, choosing instead to spend her birthday with her sister, Kathi, and Kathi's new baby.

It's hard to tell underminers that you've quit, but they're the ones who most need to hear the news. "I quit. Completely, forever, for real—get it? I'm not just cutting back; it's not a phase or an experiment. I mean it. Don't offer me drinks. Don't put a wine glass at my place at table. Don't make jokes. Don't tell me how good it tastes, or what I'm missing. If you really care about me, you'll cooperate and not undermine what I'm trying to accomplish."

Look at your list of underminers, and develop your strategy of self-protection. Figure out how you will avoid, inform, deflect, and manage each one of them. Pay special attention to your strategies for people you just won't be able to avoid seeing—people at work, for example, or nextdoor neighbors, or an ex-spouse with whom you share joint custody of your kids. In addition to the support you'll need to stay sober, you'll need support in carrying through with your determination to keep undermining influences at bay.

Sobriety Contract

An important step in quitting for good is to go on record formally with one or two very special people, such as your spouse or lover or best friend. This involves actually writing down your intentions, and spelling out how this special person will support you. Here's a sample sobriety contract you can use or adapt for your purposes:

I _____
(your name)

am quitting _____
(substance)

for good, and I want your support. I will call you immediately if I drink or use drugs again, if I feel tempted to do so, or if I just need to talk.

I _____
(supporter)

support you in your resolve not to drink or use drugs again. I expect you to call me at any time, day or night, if you drink or use drugs again, if you feel tempted to do so, or if you just need to talk. Whenever I talk to you, I will make a point of asking you how you are doing with your program of abstinence.

If it feels too strange to write down a sobriety contract, you can make a verbal agreement. The key points are

- Accepting that you can't do it alone

- Acknowledging that abstinence is your goal

- Promising to call your supporter if you slip

- Your supporter's promise to be available

- Your supporter's promise to check in regularly with you

Conclusion

If you have done the exercises so far in the book, you are probably ready to quit (or to continue in your abstinence). You will have determined the nature and severity of your problem. You'll have honestly assessed the good and bad points associated with quitting or not quitting. You'll have identified your local resources for help from medical people, support groups, and your own family and friends. You can go on to the next chapter with confidence.

If you have been skimming along without doing the exercises, just browsing to see how it all comes out, this is a key decision point. If you want to succeed in quitting, go back to Chapter 1 and do the necessary work to prepare you to quit for good.

5

Quitting

You have probably quit lots of times. Staying quit is the tough part. When alcohol and drugs get out of control, they complicate your marriage, family, work, health, finances, emotions—every part of your life. Staying quit means having to deal with all that wreckage while sober and straight.

If you mean to stay alcohol- and drug-free, it's essential for you to design a plan for yourself that will let your abstinence progress one small step at a time. Too often, people's grand intentions overreach their physical and emotional capabilities. For many people, the interval of "one day at a time" can be an eternity too long. At the beginning, you may need to think in terms of one minute at a time, and then one hour at a time, until you feel that you're able to live contentedly without drinks or drugs. You'll need to think about each block of time in terms of creating an environment conducive to your abstinence. You'll need to avoid people, places, and circumstances associated with your drinking or drug use. What constitutes a safe schedule and environment will be different for everyone; but in this chapter we'll offer some ideas that have worked well in the past for ourselves and others.

If you are already alcohol- and drug-free, great. Keep moving down that path. Just read through this chapter to find any ideas that may make it easier for you to stay on the straight and narrow.

Medical Detoxification

You should seek medical advice before trying to stop using alcohol or drugs if:

- You are over 40

- You've been drinking or using drugs regularly without a period of abstinence exceeding 72 hours

- and you have experienced significant withdrawal symptoms during past attempts at quitting

It doesn't have to hurt. There is no evidence to suggest that quitting cold turkey, with the attendant discomfort, adds to your chances for a successful recovery. There is actually research suggesting that undergoing severe withdrawal may set the neurochemical stage for panic attacks in the future.

Detoxification can be a safe and comfortable medical procedure, but it should always be done under the supervision of a trained physician. Don't go to just any doctor or facility. Inadequately trained doctors have been known to use inappropriate methods, improper dosages, and even to cross-addict people in their efforts to facilitate detoxification. Be especially careful in your choice of medical assistance if you have been using combinations of drugs and alcohol.

Call your county medical society and ask for the names of local addiction medicine specialists. Or get the name of a certified addiction specialist in your community from

American Society of Addiction Medicine
4601 North Park Ave., Suite 101
Chevy Chase, MD 20815
(301) 656-3929

Detoxification is a simple medical procedure in which the physician prescribes a short-life drug that allows the patient's nervous system to gradually and safely adjust to the absence of alcohol or other drugs. It can often be accomplished on an out-patient basis. In severe cases a brief, two- to four-day hospital stay is required.

Pick a Day and Quit

You can just pick a day and quit if

- You're under 40

- You don't drink or take drugs every day

- and you've never had severe withdrawal symptoms such as hallucinations, panic, disorientation, or "the shakes" (uncontrolled hand or body tremors)

Whether you plan to quit under medical supervision or without it, you can use the form on the next page to organize your quit day.

Quit Day Plan

My quit day: _____

What I'll do on that day instead of drinking/using drugs:

_____

_____

_____

_____

_____

_____

_____

The people I'll tell about my quit day:

_____

_____

The person or people I'll talk to if I feel bad and want to backslide:

_____

_____

Things I'll need to have on hand:
    Nonalcoholic beverages
    Nutritious food (fixings for both meals and snacks, including a few favorite treats)
    Other supplies (such as a book I want to read, music, videotapes, magazines,
        crafts projects, writing paper, a camera, a tape recorder to talk into, the
        phone numbers of my supportive contacts, a favorite photograph or picture,
        a book of affirmations, etc.)

_____

_____

_____

_____

_____

_____

_____

_____

Things I need to do before the day starts:
   Get rid of all the booze, drugs, and drug paraphernalia in my home
   Go shopping for the supplies listed above
   Other tasks (for example, see my spiritual advisor; go to confession; perform a
      ritual—go swimming, light candles, meditate; clean the house; do the laundry)

_____

_____

_____

_____

_____

_____

High-risk places and situations I'll avoid (such as people and places where I used to
drink/use drugs):

_____

_____

_____

_____

_____

Here is an example of Marcy's plan for quitting:

My quit day: Saturday, February 14

What I'll do on that day instead of drinking/using drugs:
    9:00 AA meeting
    Put all my pictures in an album
    Get a new album ready for the start of my clean and sober life
    Take my nephews ice skating
    Buy myself a special Valentine's present
    Work out at the gym, get a massage
    4:00 AA meeting
    Jerry will come over and fix dinner for us
    Watch a video with Jerry after dinner
    Light candles
    Go to bed early
    Pray

The people I'll tell about my quit day:
    Jerry
    My brother and his wife
    My sister and her husband

The person or people I'll talk to if I feel bad and want to backslide:
    Jerry
    My sister

Things I'll need to have on hand:
    My ice skates and warm clothes
    Box of photos, new albums
    Exercise clothes
    Videotape for watching after dinner
    Healthy snack foods, stuff for breakfast and lunch (Jerry will bring ingredients
        for dinner); lots of juice and mineral water
    Candles

Things I need to do before the day starts:
    Dump out all the bourbon bottles in the house and garage
    Gather up all the bottles in my wine cellar and give them to Dinah—she can use
        them for her restaurant (but don't spend time with Dinah!)
    Go shopping for groceries

Buy the new photo albums
Rent a videotape
Make the date with the kids to take them skating
Make an appointment for the massage
Make sure I have clean clothes
Straighten up the house
Join an athletic club
Take up a sport I once played
Call Janie, Dave, and Jerry

High-risk places and situations I'll avoid:
I won't go out to any restaurants or cafes or bars(!) where alcohol is served
I won't see Mom, Dodie, Anne, Bonnie, Mark, or Paula, and I won't talk to them
on the phone (I'll screen my calls)
I won't feel sorry for myself (if I do, I'll call Janie or Jerry immediately!)

Use the same format to plan your second straight and sober day. And your third. And your fourth. In the beginning, this is what "one day at a time" means—literally planning every minute of sobriety so that you avoid high-risk situations, keep occupied, and reinforce your recovery at every turn.

For more and longer-term strategies, see Chapter 12, "Relapse Prevention."

Finding the Magic

It is possible for you to quit and live happily without alcohol and drugs. Countless addicted people, who tried many times and in every way they could think of to quit, eventually found the "magic" that allowed them to succeed. What happened? What did they do, think, or feel that made everything finally change? More to the point, how can you tap into their formula? Let's begin by examining possible approaches and likely results.

Taking charge. "I'm taking control of my life. I've made my decision, and that's that." This attitude rarely works. You won't hear many recovery success stories that involve conquering, overcoming, taking charge, and so on. It's clear that efforts to deal with addictions by means of sheer willpower usually fail. There are always exceptions; and you may be able to judge whether you yourself are an exception to the rule by looking at any past attempts you've made at quitting.

Insight and enlightenment. "At last I understand why I do this! Now I won't have to do it any more." If ignorance or stupidity caused addiction, then it would make sense that knowledge would be the cure. However, the rolls of brilliant people who have died of alcohol and drug dependencies are sad testimony that you can't outsmart this condition. Addiction occurs in the instinctual part of the brain, where reason and knowledge have little effect.

Humility and surrender. "I'm beginning to see how bad things have become, how much I have hurt people. I see that others still care about me. I see that there is a way out with dignity. I am willing to get help." It is from a position of humility that most successful recovery stories begin. Go to an AA meeting and you'll hear recovering alcoholics use all sorts of paradoxical phrases about the payoff from humble acceptance of their powerlessness: "When I admitted my powerlessness, I felt empowered," or "By surrendering, I was able to win."

All this sounds like giving up—not the sort of thing that appeals to most people. But when you accept your powerlessness over drugs and alcohol, all you are really saying is that none of your previous efforts to stop have worked. It is time to let go of the old ways, and to open yourself to new ideas.

"Surrender" is really the wrong word to describe what happens when you truly accept the pathological nature of your addiction. "Profound redirection of energy" would be a more accurate description of what occurs. When you're drinking and using drugs, you must expend an enormous amount of mental and physical energy to handle the continual crises associated with that lifestyle. Any reflection on the past brings painful remorse, and looking to the future produces fear and anxiety.

When you "surrender," you let go of all that chaos, and focus entirely on strategies to keep you from taking the next drink or hit of your drug. You redirect your mental and physical energy away from all that crisis management and emotional turmoil, and towards the positive goal of sober and straight living. This is the profound shift that is consistently reported by those who successfully recover.

You may ask, "Isn't that just willpower by another name?" No, because acceptance leading to change feels very different from taking charge and trying to make change happen. This is not a word game. It is a distinction of life-and-death significance. Many people die trying to take charge, control, manage, or otherwise out-muscle their addictions. On the other hand, hundreds find recovery every day through the profound act of accepting their pathological powerlessness over alcohol and drugs.

You can liken acceptance versus taking charge to the difference between western-style boxing or wrestling and eastern martial arts, such as aikido, kung fu, or karate. The boxer or wrestler often tries to overcome his opponent with brute strength. The martial arts expert accepts the fact that his opponent may be stronger than he. He moves with, rather than against, the forces opposing him, co-opting their strength. He deflects his opponents' energy, directing it back at him.

If you accept your powerlessness over addictive substances, the energy you might have spent trying to control your dependence becomes available to fuel your recovery efforts. As foreign as acceptance, surrender, letting go, and opening up to new ways of living may feel, these concepts contain the magic ingredient that will allow you to quit with success.

What Can Stop You?

Once you have rid yourself of all addictive substances, all you have to do is not take the next drink or drug. Sounds simple, but addiction is a disease characterized by relapse. Early relapses are caused by four conditions, separately or in combination with each other:

- Physical craving for alcohol or drugs

- Psychological longing for the euphoria associated with alcohol or drugs

- Physical pain which you hope to relieve with alcohol or drugs

- Emotional pain which you hope to relieve with alcohol or drugs

Here are some suggestions for avoiding or coping with each of these conditions.

Physical Craving

The prevailing theory is that physical craving for alcohol or other drugs is caused by deficiencies in one or more of the neurotransmitters—brain chemicals normally associated with feelings of well-being, pleasure, and euphoria. This explanation tracks well with the actual experiences of people who describe craving drink or drugs to "feel normal," to "get relief," to "get comfortable," or to "feel less depressed."

These kinds of feelings are fueled by brain chemicals. If your genes, or past alcohol and drug exposure, have created deficiencies in neurotransmitters, you will crave the restorative powers of your drug of choice, especially soon after you've quit, and all the drug is out of your system. This is when the new craving-blocker drugs such as *Revia*™ can be helpful.

If this condition were permanent, most addicted people would never recover. Fortunately, time does heal. Physical cravings usually fade away in a few days or weeks. Perhaps the brain chemicals, their receptors, or the release mechanisms partially restore themselves. No one knows for sure. What is certain is that you will not have to go through life wrestling with intense physical cravings. They will pass. And unless you resurrect the craving by taking a drink or drug, it will not return—at least not in the same powerful and overwhelming way.

To handle physical cravings, make sure that your first few days after quitting are fully planned to avoid high-risk situations, and to include lots of support from AA, therapists, friends, family, and so on.

Physical craving can also be triggered by accidental exposure to alcohol or other addictive substances in some mouthwashes, cough medicines, painkillers, and prescription drugs. Read labels carefully; when in doubt, leave the substance out of your body. Most experts also advise not drinking so-called de-alcoholized wines or nonalcoholic beers, because they do contain a trace of alcohol that can trigger cravings. In addition, the familiar wine and beer bottles can provide psychological cues leading to relapse.

Eating regular, well-balanced meals, getting plenty of rest and moderate exercise will maximize your physical health, speed your physical detoxification, and reduce physical cravings. See the next chapter, "Nutrition and Exercise."

Psychological Craving

This is another kind of craving that stems from the memory of the "good times" associated with past alcohol or drug use. It is easier to recall the euphoric feelings of the past than to honestly examine the unpleasant behaviors and events that may have accompanied them. Such distorted recollection can trigger powerful longings for the good old days. Cues picked up from people, places, activities, music, even certain foods can rekindle the desire for alcohol or drugs.

The way to keep this fire banked is to acknowledge that alcohol and drugs no longer do for you what they once did; and that the so-called good times frequently resulted in pain for others. An honest look will reveal that past fun was often at the expense of time, money, and attention that could have been better spent on family, friends, work, and community. Review your work from Chapter 3 on the drawbacks of continuing to drink or take drugs.

Nevertheless, breaking up the chemical love affair is very much a case of grieving the loss of what was once a source of pleasure. In these early days of recovery, you'll need to keep telling yourself that those days really are gone forever. And you'll need to have lots of positive and pleasant alternative activities planned to keep you busy.

For example, Daniel belonged to a veterans' group that met every Friday for happy hour. He hadn't been going since he stopped drinking. One Friday after work, he was feeling at loose ends, and replaying the great times he had with his drinking buddies. Daniel was wise enough to call John, a more experienced recovering friend. John helped him to see that those "good times" involved spending money that his family needed, and taking time away from his roles as husband, father, and good citizen. The jokes at happy hour were usually at the expense of some person or group, and the clever, sparkling conversation actually sounded pretty stupid when replayed in sober retrospect.

Daniel managed to shake off nostalgia, hired a babysitter, and invited his wife out to see a movie and have dinner at her favorite restaurant. The result was reinforced recovery, no hangover on Saturday morning, a sense of satisfaction, and a grateful spouse.

Physical Pain

In the early days of recovery, physical pain and discomfort can become intense, sabotaging your efforts to quit. Asked how you are feeling in the first few days, you might honestly reply, "I am over- (or under-) weight, sick to my stomach, tired out; my head hurts, and my hands shake. I'm jittery and restless."

Hopefully all that is not true for you at one time. Still, you may feel terrible, assailed by bouts of physical symptoms from which you can no longer escape through alcohol or other drugs.

It will help a little to remind yourself that physical pain is a normal component of being alive. It might well be said, "I hurt, therefore I am." Illness is a fact of existence, and injuries are the price of motion. Try to learn the lessons of patience and tolerance that ordinary aches and pains can teach.

It will also help to realize that alcohol and drugs are toxic substances, and that physical pain in the early stages of your recovery will probably fade as your system detoxifies.

When tempted to have a little drink, snort, or pill to ease the pain, remember that, in the long run, more alcohol and drugs will mean more pain.

Do the exercises in the next chapter on nutrition and exercise. Good food, rest, and moderate exercise will eventually relieve much of your discomfort.

If you are truly sick or injured, go to the doctor. At least you no longer have to worry that he or she will tell you to stop drinking. In most cases, there will be an effective nonalcoholic, nonaddictive treatment to give you relief. It's almost always easier to deal with the known than the open-ended fear of the unknown—so do get a professional diagnosis if you're worried by a medical problem.

For example, years ago Walter hurt his back helping a friend move, and had been bothered by recurring pain in his lower back ever since. Once in a while he forgot to be careful, and his back went out. In his drinking days, Walter used to treat the pain with a couple of *Darvon* and Irish whisky. He was sure that he had a bad disk, and would need surgery. When he stopped drinking, his back pain became constantly annoying and sometimes very painful. He longed for relief, but feared going to the doctor because he was certain it would mean painful surgery.

Finally it became a question of starting to drink again or seeing the doc. Walter's recovering friends convinced him to have his back checked—he would always have the choice about whether to have recourse to surgery. To his relief and surprise, Walter learned he had a weak muscle that he kept re-injuring. The doctor told him to take Ibuprofen, and referred him for physical therapy, which permanently cured his back pain.

Emotional Pain

This is the biggie. Emotional pain is one of the legacies of long-term alcohol and drug use. If you have done things under the influence that violated your own rules of behavior, then you are no doubt paying the price of guilt, shame, and remorse. Wasted years and loss of loved ones, relationships, health, money, or reputation can lead to depression. Anger at yourself and others can flare up easily. You may be deathly afraid of relapse. Yet the prospect of facing the rest of your life straight and sober also makes you extremely anxious.

In the early days of recovery, you must keep reminding yourself that painful emotions are perfectly normal. Having them doesn't mean you're bad or crazy or going to die. You're on the same emotional roller coaster that thousands have ridden before you. Your first goal is just to hang on and not do anything rash, such as drink, drug, or otherwise harm yourself. Eventually the roller coaster will slow down.

When emotional pain peaks, it's important to always have someone supportive you can call, some safe place you can go, some positive activity you can do, or something inspirational or reassuring you can read. That's why you need to plan the day when you quit, and the first few days of recovery, so carefully.

Because the early days are bound to be emotional, try to avoid making any big decisions then about money, jobs, relationships, moving, and so on. Wait until you have a few months of sobriety under your belt, and the storms of emotion have subsided a bit.

Most of the remaining chapters in this book are about achieving the emotional maturity and stability you need for long-term recovery. If anxiety is your main symptom, see Chapter 7, which discusses relaxation. Chapter 8, on feelings will help you control resentment and anger; get you in touch with more elusive feelings, such as sadness; and help you with the appropriate expression of all your feelings. To get started on relieving guilt and remorse, move on to Chapter 9, which deals with spirituality. Chapters 10 and 11 on communication and making amends, continue the process of repairing damaged relationships and making new ones that are emotionally sound.

6

Nutrition and Exercise

Accepting responsibility is an important part of recovery. That includes accepting responsibility for your own body. Accepting responsibility for your body means developing a sense of *stewardship* for it. Stewardship implies love, respect, observation, appreciation, and careful tending of something valuable and complex that has been put in your charge. Just as a farmer can exercise stewardship of a plot of land, or a caretaker can be the steward of a rare historical building or collection of heirlooms, you can practice stewardship of your body.

You only have one body. It's unique, different from everyone else's. It is your most precious possession, a true heirloom passed down to you from your ancestors. You need to take good care of your body, especially considering the harmful chemicals you have carelessly put into it in the past.

This chapter will show you how to develop the habit of eating a healthier, more balanced diet. It will get you started on a program of regular exercise to increase your endurance, strength, and flexibility. Nutrition and exercise are both important when you have recently quit alcohol or other drugs. By eating well and exercising, you can:

- Repair the damage that drugs and alcohol have done to your body

- Improve your mental clarity

- Establish regular habits to support a life that's free of chemical dependencies

- Reach and maintain a healthy weight

- Restore your zest for living

- Increase your energy level

- Raise your self-esteem

- Reduce your stress level

- Prevent future illness

Nutrition

Most chemically dependent people have bad eating habits that deliver inadequate nutrition. It's not surprising, since by definition chemical dependency means that you're not good at controlling what you put into your body. You may consume too much fat, caffeine, sugar, salt, and preservatives. You probably don't eat enough whole grains, fresh fruit, and vegetables. Your diet might lack variety and, therefore, certain essential vitamins and minerals. You may snack all day, or forget to eat entirely.

When you quit drinking or taking other drugs, you will probably continue in or aggravate your bad eating habits. A look around a typical AA meeting will show you how many people fall back on coffee, cigarettes, and sweets when they let go of their favorite treat—alcohol.

You may feel that, having given up a life-destroying substance like bourbon or crack, you can indulge yourself with a Twinkie or a Big Mac now and then. And you can, for a while. No one ever got busted for driving under the influence of a cheese Danish, or blacked out after downing three orders of french fries.

But, in the long term, most recovering people report that it is easier to resist cravings for alcohol and drugs if you gradually learn to curb your cravings for sugar, fat, and salt. Your long-term goal should be to reach maximum health by gradually getting your diet under control. Start right now by beginning a daily food diary. This will record a baseline of how and what you currently eat. Make photocopies of the diary page if you would like to record your eating habits over more than three days.

Daily Food Diary

Day 1

Meal (or snack)	Food (How much?)	Where Consumed	What Else Were You Doing at the Time?	Feelings

Day 2

Meal (or snack)	Food (How much?)	Where Consumed	What Else Were You Doing at the Time?	Feelings

Day 3

Meal (or snack)	Food (How much?)	Where Consumed	What Else Were You Doing at the Time?	Feelings

Note that there is space for recording where you were when eating, what else you were doing at the time (such as reading, watching TV, driving, talking on the phone), and how you were feeling. That's because there may be certain places, activities, and feelings associated with your eating habits. In order to change your habits, you may have to avoid certain settings, or learn to notice your feelings and deal with them in some way other than eating.

Here's an example of how Caroline filled out her diary on a typical day:

Meal (or Snack)	Food (How much?)	Where Consumed	What Else Were You Doing at the Time?	Feelings
Breakfast	1/2 cup Granola 1 cup whole milk 2 cups black coffee	Kitchen	Reading paper	Rushed, nervous
Snack	2 donuts 2 cups coffee	My desk at work	Reading reports	Busy, irritated
Snack	1 bag cornuts 1 chocolate milk 1 cup coffee	My desk at work (missed lunch)		Hungry, resentful
Dinner	9 Chicken nuggets large chocolate shake large fries 1 piece cherry pie 1 cup coffee	McDonalds	Nothing	Tired, depressed; (afterwards) bloated
Snack	5 cookies 2 cups coffee	AA meeting	Talking, listening	Safe, relieved

Caroline tended to ignore what she ate. She felt tired and stressed out much of the time. She often missed breakfast or lunch, then filled up on too much starchy food when she got a chance. She ate out at fast food joints, or out of the food vending machines at work. She drank six or seven cups of coffee a day. She used food to console herself when depressed, to celebrate when she felt happy, or to soothe herself when she felt stressed or angry. In fact, she used food the same way she used to use vodka and *Percodan*.

After keeping your food diary for three days, compare what you typically eat with this recommended balanced diet:

At every meal

Mostly complex carbohydrates, such as whole grain breads, pasta, rice, and cereals; at least one fresh vegetable or fruit, preferably raw or lightly cooked

At one meal a day

Protein source, such as lean meat, chicken, fish, or beans

To avoid or only eat rarely

Fatty, salty, fried, or sugary foods, like ice cream, donuts, fried chicken, cheeseburgers, bacon, candy bars, potato chips, whole-milk dairy products, oils, and egg yolks

If you're like most chemically dependent people, your diet is probably the opposite of the recommended one. You eat lots of what you should eat only rarely. You may have meat or dairy products at almost every meal. When you do have rice or pasta, they're smothered in meaty sauces or cheese. Your fruits and vegetables, far from being fresh, are likely to show up in the form of strawberries in a fast-food strawberry milk shake, or the apples in an apple pie.

What should you do? Where to start? You can't just suddenly begin eating like a Zen monk from now on. It's too big a change. Your body and your mind will rebel.

Fortunately, improving nutrition can be done gradually, one step at a time. It's different from giving up alcohol or drugs, where complete abstinence is the goal. Food is different. You have to keep eating. While you're eating, you can work toward moderation. You can modify one eating behavior at a time.

To help you form a plan for improving your nutrition, here are eight steps you can choose from. The most important steps are listed first. The less important, or less commonly applicable steps, are listed toward the end. Start with Step 1 and stick with it until you have developed some new habits. Then go on to Step 2 and work on that for a while. Then Step 3, and so on.

Eight Steps Toward Better Eating

1. Reduce Your Intake of Fat

Americans eat about 40 percent of their calories in the form of fat, rather than the recommended 25 percent. Start reading labels on all the prepared food you buy. Look for items with fewer than three grams of fat per serving. Stay away from fast food, like burgers and tacos. Be skeptical—the chicken dishes at most fast-food chains are fried in beef fat. You're not always eating what you think you're eating.

Read labels on *everything*. Fat lurks where you least expect it: in chips that seem dry as dust, in flaky pie crust, in salad dressings and other condiments. Products marked "Reduced Fat" can still be tremendously fattening. Oils marked "No cholesterol" are still fatty (cholesterol is only found in animal products, such as butter, meat, and eggs).

Your best bet is to avoid packaged or fast foods altogether. Then you can *know* what you're eating. If you're not used to doing much cooking, check out the cookbook section in your public library, or look for a cooking class that focuses on low-fat meals. Talk to friends who look fit and healthy, and find out what *they're* eating.

2. *Reduce Your Intake of Sugar*

The average American eats 130 pounds of sugar a year. If you're an alcoholic, you're probably used to more than your share, since alcohol contains a lot of sugar. A sweet treat gives a quick high that's not as good as alcohol or stronger drugs, but better than nothing when you're hurting. But like any mood-altering substance, there is an inevitable downside.

Sugar gives you a little rush of energy, but it also stimulates your pancreas to produce insulin, which eats up the sugar in your blood until you're a little hypoglycemic. This low blood sugar level makes you feel tired, hungry, maybe irritable or nauseated. It inspires you to seek more sugar.

So use less sugar, honey, and syrup. Cut way back on candy, cookies, cake, pie, and soda pop. Try eating fresh fruit when you crave something sweet. Read labels, and avoid anything that lists among its first four ingredients *sucrose, glucose, maltose, dextrose, lactose, or fructose* (these are all different names for sugar).

3. *Avoid Caffeine*

Caffeine is a powerful stimulant that would probably be available only by prescription if the FDA reviewed it today as a new drug.

Caffeine is found in coffee, black tea, cola, some medicines, and chocolate. Regular brewed coffee has the most. Instant coffee and black tea have about half as much caffeine as brewed coffee. A small bar of dark chocolate or a cup of cola have about half as much caffeine as a cup of black tea.

Taper off coffee, tea, and chocolate by gradually switching to decaffeinated coffee and tea, and herbal infusions (a lot of these are very coffee- or tea-like without the caffeine). Again, when you feel in need of a lift, eat some fresh fruit, get some fresh air and exercise, or take a nap!

4. *Reduce Your Intake of Salt*

While you're reading those labels, look out for foods that list salt or sodium high in their list of ingredients. Sodium is an essential mineral found in table salt and many foods. You need some sodium to stay alive, but Americans eat way too much. Excess sodium can contribute to high blood pressure, increased risk of stroke, retaining water, and aggravated PMS.

Cut back on chips, pretzels, salted nuts, soy sauce, pickles, cheese, sausage, and bacon. Cut the addition of salt in half when you cook, and don't put the salt shaker on the table. Try lemon juice, herbs, and spices instead of salt to lend savor to foods.

5. *Take a Multivitamin Tablet Daily*

Vitamins and minerals are essential micronutrients. Taking a multivitamin tablet each day is good insurance for several reasons:

- Alcohol and other drugs deplete your body of certain vitamins

- You're covered on those days when you don't eat a perfectly balanced diet

- It can make up for vitamins lost or destroyed in food processing

- The stress of overcoming your chemical dependency may cause you to need extra vitamins

Don't go overboard. Too much of some vitamins—such as too much Vitamin A—can be toxic to your liver, cause diarrhea, increase the risk of kidney stones, and so on. Stick to a single, high-quality tablet a day. Or get some advice from a nutritionist or someone at a health-food store if you plan to take an array of vitamins. If you have serious medical problems, such as impaired liver or kidney function, let your physician know about your plans to use vitamin supplements.

6. Eat a Variety of Foods

This is really a summary step, to check how you are doing. If you have reduced your intake of fat, sugar, caffeine, and salt, you should already have introduced greater variety into your diet. Varying your diet is the best way to make sure you get all of the 40 different nutrients your body needs to survive. Each day make sure you have something from these main food groups:

- Bread, rice, cereal, pasta: 6-11 half-cup servings

- Fruits and vegetables: equivalent of 5 half-cup servings

- Meat, chicken, fish, low-fat dairy products, beans: equivalent of 2 half-cup servings

7. Choose More Complex Carbohydrates

Some of the nervousness that goes with early sobriety can be eased by eating foods with adequate starch and fiber, such as whole-grain breads, bran cereals, brown rice, fresh fruits, and vegetables. These sources of carbohydrates act like natural tranquilizers. They contain tryptophan, an amino acid that stimulates your brain to produce serotonin, which has a calming effect. The high fiber content aids digestion, prevents constipation, and may guard against colon cancer.

8. Eat Frequent, Calm Meals

Don't skip meals. Consider that five small meals a day might be better for you than three larger ones. Eating frequently will smooth out peaks and valleys in your blood sugar level and your mood.

Take the time to prepare good food. Eat it slowly and with enjoyment and appreciation. Plan ahead by shopping for several days at a time. Plan to have leftovers for lunches and other meals on busy days. Reheated leftovers are better for you than grabbing fast food. At work, try to take time out for a relaxed meal.

Again, don't go overboard with this step. It is not intended as permission to snack compulsively all day long. Eat when you're hungry, and stop eating when you no longer feel hungry. This sounds deceptively simple. Many people are so habituated to eat when it's mealtime that they have forgotten what hunger feels like. They may also eat too quickly or unconsciously to recognize when they feel full. Try to just eat—or, better yet, eat and converse—while you're eating. Don't read, don't watch TV, don't eat in your car. Talking with friends or family during a meal will slow you down and make the meal last longer and feel more satisfying.

Caroline began with Step 1 and set out to reduce fat in her diet. She baked chicken breasts at home, and ate them with a salad, a baked potato, and lemonade instead of getting a cheeseburger and shake at a fast-food restaurant. She took apples and bananas to eat at work instead of hitting the machine for cornuts and chips. The fresh fruit also replaced her morning donut when she started working on Step 2, reducing her intake of sugar.

Caroline took six months to make any real progress on caffeine. She finally found an herbal tea that she liked, and started carrying tea bags around in her purse so she could brew some whenever she was offered coffee.

Two years later, Caroline was taking vitamins and eating a varied diet at home more often. She described herself as "not exactly a health nut, but a conscious eater." She felt better, was 12 pounds lighter, had become good at cooking many oriental dishes, and actually grew some of her own vegetables each summer in her garden.

Daily reminders

To help you work on your nutrition steps, carry an index card or a small notebook with you. Jot down what you eat each day, and review your record before you go to sleep at night. That way you'll stay conscious of how you are eating, and will have an opportunity to set a goal for improvement each day.

Exercise

Good nutrition and regular exercise go together. People need both for optimum health. If you have recently quit drugs and alcohol, you especially need to eat right and exercise carefully to maximize your recovery.

If you're over 30, have a family history of heart disease, are more than 25 percent overweight, take medications, or suffer from any chronic disease, it is a good idea to consult your doctor before beginning an exercise program.

There are basically three types of exercise: aerobic, stretching, and toning.

Aerobic Exercise

This is the type of exercise that will do you the most good. Aerobic exercises involve vigorous, sustained use of your large muscles, especially your legs. This gets your heart beating fast, and makes it stronger.

To strengthen your heart, you need at least 20 minutes of aerobic exercise, three times a week. The exercise should be fairly intense, so that your heart rate stays high for the whole 20 minutes. Ideal aerobic heart rates vary with age and fitness level. A good range is from 60 to 75 percent of the maximum rate your heart is capable of beating. The following chart will help you find your target heart rate.

Aerobic Heart Rates

Age	Target Heart Rate—Heartbeats per minute
20–24	120–150
25–29	117–146
30–34	113–142
35–39	111–138
40–44	108–135
45–49	105–131
50–54	102–127
55–59	99–123
60–64	96–120
65–69	93–116
70+	90–113

To measure your heart rate, exercise for five minutes, then take your pulse in your wrist or your neck. Count how many times your heart beats in ten seconds. Multiply this by six to get the rate per minute.

If you're in pretty good shape, shoot for the higher end of the range for your age group. If you're out of shape and just beginning to exercise, shoot for the lower end of the range. Take it easy. Too much intensity is worse than not enough—it will put a strain on your heart instead of strengthening it.

Choose an aerobic exercise from this list:

☐ Running

☐ Bicycling

☐ Fast walking

☐ Rowing

☐ Dancing

☐ Cross country skiing

☐   Racquetball

☐   Tennis (singles)

☐   Swimming

☐   Jumping rope

☐   Basketball

☐   Dancing

☐   Skating

☐   Stair climbing

☐   Step aerobics

☐   Jazzercise

Most of these activities can be done "for real" or in modified versions indoors in a gym or at home, on rowing machines, stair steppers, treadmills, and so on. Pick one or two, and schedule your next week's aerobic exercise:

	Monday	Tuesday	Wednesday	Thursday	Friday	Saturday	Sunday
Time:	_____	_____	_____	_____	_____	_____	_____
Place:	_____	_____	_____	_____	_____	_____	_____

If you plan to exercise every other day, you can miss a day and still get in three sessions per week.

Reality Check—Start Slowly

This section of the chapter has been barreling along as if you were an average person who had been living a quiet, sedentary life and wanted to jump into an exercise program and whip the old bod into shape. If you fit this profile, learn to listen to your own body as you launch into an exercise program.

But what if you've been living the wild life of drinking, drugs, late nights, bad food, no food, fist fights, sleeping in your car, killer hangovers, blackouts, passing out, drunk driving, vomiting blood, falling down? In that case, the old bod is not going to respond well to a sudden increase in activity. You may be feeling so shaky and fragile that you're not ready for exercise yet.

If you've been abusing your body, you need to go to a physician and get advice about how soon and how hard to exercise. Start slowly. Your ideal thrice-weekly aerobic workout may be a slow shuffle once around the block.

When you do exercise, be aware of what's going on in your body. If you get so short of breath that you can't carry on a conversation while exercising, you're overdoing it. Pull back a little. If your joints and muscles hurt while exercising, slow down. If you're over 40, seriously consider the lower-impact forms of aerobics, like brisk walking or swimming. Jogging or running may be too hard on your knees and ankles.

Chemically dependent people tend to have an all-or-nothing approach to life that tells them "if a little is good, then a lot more is better." Don't fall for that line of thinking and overdo your exercise.

Stretching and Toning

Stretching is just what it sounds like—stretching muscles and tendons so that they are longer, more flexible, and warmed by extra blood circulation.

Toning is the opposite—contracting muscles so that they become stronger with use. Toning exercises are weight lifting, calisthenics, isotonics, and isometrics. At this point in your exercise program, you don't need to do specific toning exercises. You will get all the toning you need in the course of stretching and doing your aerobic exercise.

You should always stretch your muscles before doing aerobic exercise. When your muscles are stretched and warm, it's easier and safer to exercise aerobically. You're a lot less likely to injure yourself running or playing tennis, for example, if you stretch first.

Stretching is also important *after* aerobic exercise, to relax muscles that may have become tight with repeated contractions.

On pages 70 and 71 are three stretching exercises that will prepare your whole body for aerobic exercise, or help cool and relax you afterwards.

Example

Calvin was a heating and air conditioning contractor who had been a heavy drinker for 25 years. When he quit at age 42, he was 50 pounds overweight, had poor lung capacity, chronic gastritis and heartburn, and a bad back.

When Calvin got out of the 28-day in-patient program, his doctor told him that he needed to stay off alcohol, eat low fat, high fiber foods, and start a cautious exercise program. Cal began by walking the six blocks from his house to his construction yard instead of driving his truck each morning. He would pick up his phone messages, meet with his crew chiefs, and then walk back to his house to get his truck. He would spend five minutes doing stretching exercises before setting off each day, and when he got back to the house.

The first morning, Cal walked at a slow pace for five minutes and took his pulse for ten seconds while still walking. Multiplying by six, it came to 100 beats per minute—less than the 115 that he had set as his target. So he speeded up a bit until his heart was working at 115 beats per minute.

After several weeks, Cal had to walk quite briskly to keep his heart rate up to 115. He started walking by a longer route that took ten minutes each way. Then he added a 20-minute

Stretching Exercises

A. Side body stretch. (1) Stand erect, arms at sides, feet shoulder width apart, and legs relaxed with knees slightly bent. (2) Raise one arm over your head to the side. Keeping stomach tucked in and chest high, continue to bend your arm and trunk to the side until you feel a stretch in your waist. Hold this position for five seconds. (3) Return to starting position. (4) Repeat on the other side. *Begin with five repetitions on each side.*

figure A-1   figure A-2

figure A-3   figure A-4

Reprinted with permission from *The Relaxation & Stress Reduction Workbook*, Davis et al., New Harbinger Publications.

B. Leg and back stretch. (1) Stand with feet together, arms at sides, and eyes looking straight ahead. (2) Squat down, keeping heels on floor and reaching your arms straight ahead. Hold ten seconds. (3) Reach hands forward between knees and slide body forward onto knees. (4) Continue sliding forward until front of body touches floor. (5) With hands on floor in front of shoulders, press chest away from floor by straightening elbows. Keep front of hips in contact with floor. Keep head and neck relaxed, eyes looking at the floor. Hold ten seconds. (6) Push back into the squatting position. Hold for another ten seconds. (7) Return to starting position. *Begin with five repetitions.*

C. Full body stretch. (1) Lie on the floor with legs straight and arms overhead. (2) Stretch right arm and leg in opposite directions. Hold five seconds. (3) Stretch left arm and left leg in opposite directions. Hold five seconds. (4) Stretch left arm and right leg in opposite directions. Hold five seconds. (5) Stretch right arm and left leg in opposite directions. Hold five seconds. (6) Stretch both arms and legs in opposite directions. Hold five seconds. *Begin with five repetitions.*

figure B-1

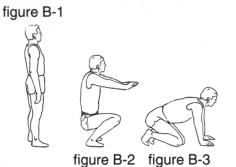

figure B-2   figure B-3

figure C-1   figure C-2   figure C-3

figure B-4

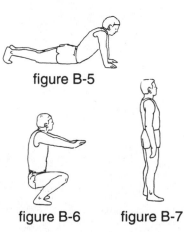

figure B-5

figure B-6   figure B-7

figure C-4   figure C-5   figure C-6

Reprinted with permission from *The Relaxation & Stress Reduction Workbook*, Davis et al., New Harbinger Publications.

walk every other evening. In six months, he was having to walk very fast, almost jogging, to keep his heart at the target level. He had lost 30 pounds by then, and felt almost light on his feet.

Cal began to alternate 50 steps of walking and 50 steps of jogging. Eventually he could do a slow jog for most of the 20 minutes.

The jogging hurt his knees, so Cal cut out the evening jogs, and joined a gym that had a stair-stepper machine. He also did a little work on the lower back machine to strengthen his stomach muscles. Losing weight and strengthening his stomach muscles almost completely cured his bad back.

Forty pounds lighter, sober for over a year, Cal took some time off and went to Jamaica with his new girlfriend. He didn't feel embarrassed being seen in his swimming trunks—in fact, he thought he must be looking pretty good, judging by the way some of the women were giving him the eye. He felt so good, so strong, that he celebrated with a little taste of the local rum. That was the beginning of a three-month relapse for Calvin, during which he reverted to heavy drinking, fatty food, and no exercise.

When he finally quit booze again, this time for good, part of the impetus was how bad his body felt. Cal had become accustomed to regular exercise, and his body seemed to miss it in every cell of every muscle.

7

Relaxation

Chemically dependent people react to stress by reaching for their drug of choice. This chapter will teach you how to relax without drugs or alcohol.

You experience stress from many sources. Your immediate environment presents you with bad weather, noise, traffic, mechanical breakdowns, and pollution. Your relationships with others stress you with arguments, deadlines, unwanted commitments, financial problems, legal hassles, and temptations to drink or use drugs. Your own body stresses you with illness, accidents, pain, aging, menopause in women, poor nutrition, lack of exercise, and fatigue.

If you've recently stopped consuming alcohol and other drugs, you experience additional stress from withdrawal symptoms, physical damage you may have done to your body, and the loss of your old addictive lifestyle.

Fight or Flight

Around the turn of the century, a Harvard physiologist named Walter B. Cannon described the mind and body's response to stress as the "fight-or-flight" response. This is a four-step process:

1. The conscious level of your brain perceives a situation as dangerous or unpleasant.

2. A message is sent from your higher brain levels to your brain stem.

3. Your brain stem excites the nerves that regulate your digestion, heartbeat, glands, and the dilation of your blood vessels.

4. Your breathing and heart rate increase. Your liver releases stored sugar to nourish your muscles. Your blood pressure rises. The blood vessels in your hands and feet and digestive system contract, so that your blood pools in your heart, and in the

vessels serving your large muscles and your central nervous system. Your glands release adrenaline and other hormones that make your body ready to move fast, reduce your sensitivity to pain, and depress your immune system.

Many of the techniques in this book teach you to change your perception of the stressful events in your life, so that you perceive fewer situations as threatening, and therefore trigger the fight-or-flight response less frequently. However, this chapter concentrates on the purely physical reactions to stress, and shows you how to relax once the fight-or-flight response has begun.

Progressive Muscle Relaxation

This technique acts quickly and directly on the symptoms of stress by loosening tight muscles. Progressive muscle relaxation is frequently recommended to relieve chronic muscular tension, insomnia, fatigue, irritable bowel, muscle spasms, neck and back pain, and high blood pressure.

Muscle relaxation also relieves painful emotions and cravings. While you are completely relaxed, it's impossible to feel emotions such as fear, anxiety, depression, or anger. It's also impossible to feel strong cravings for alcohol or drugs when you are profoundly relaxed. Feelings and cravings depend on a minimum level of physical arousal before they can be felt. This is the basis of relaxation's great calming effect. It returns you to a natural balance, a centered state of homeostasis in which your mind is at peace and your body can heal itself. The procedure is easy. You start with your arms, tensing the various muscles, noticing what that feels like, then relaxing the muscles and noticing what relaxation feels like. You go on to do the same thing with the muscles associated with your head, then your torso, and finally your legs. You focus on each muscle group at least twice, with more repetitions for especially tense areas.

Fifteen minutes, twice a day is the recommended schedule. In one or two weeks you should be able to reach deep levels of relaxation fairly quickly. You will come to know which muscles need more relaxation, and you'll be very sensitive to the buildup of tension in your body. After you've mastered the basic procedure, you'll probably want to mostly use the shorthand version that is outlined later.

You can try to remember these instructions and follow them with your eyes closed. A better approach the first few times is to tape record them, so that you can listen to them with your eyes closed. Speak slowly and clearly, in a calm voice. Where you see a notation such as "(5 sec)" in the script, pause for a count of five seconds before going on.

PMR Script

Lie down on your back on a couch, bed, or the floor. Find a comfortable position with your arms and legs uncrossed. You can put a pillow under your knees to take the strain off your lower back. Close your eyes gently.

Now clench your right fist, tighter and tighter, studying the tension as you hold your hand tightly in a fist. Keep it clenched, and notice the tension in your fist, wrist, and forearm. Keep the muscles tight just a little longer . . . Now relax.

Feel the looseness in your right hand, and notice the contrast with the tension. Concentrate on the feeling of relaxation for a moment. (5 sec)

Try it again. Clench your right fist again, as tight as you can without hurting yourself. Study the feeling of muscular tension in your fist, your wrist, and your forearm . . . Now relax. Feel the contrast as relaxation floods into your muscles. Notice the difference between tension and relaxation for a moment. (5 sec)

Now do the same thing with your left fist. Curl your left hand into a fist and hold it tightly. Keep it clenched and notice the tension in your hand, your wrist, and your forearm. Hold the tightness . . . hold it . . . and relax. Feel the looseness in your left hand now, notice how relaxation feels different from tension. Keep focused on the feeling in your left hand for another moment. (5 sec)

Clench your left hand again, very tightly, but not so tight that it hurts. Study the feeling of tension in your forearm, your wrist, and your hand . . . now relax. Feel the contrast between the tension and the relaxation. Notice whether your muscles feel heavy, or warm, or tingling. Stay focused on the sensations of relaxation for a moment. (5 sec)

Now try it with both fists at once. Curl both hands into fists and clench them firmly. Hold the tension and notice how hard and tight they feel . . . now relax both fists at once. Feel the relaxation flow down your arms and into the muscles and joints of your forearms, your wrists, and your hands. Study this feeling of slack, loose relaxation for a moment. (5 sec)

Next, bend both your arms at the elbows and tense your biceps. Hold your upper arms as tightly flexed as you can. Notice what this feels like. Notice if it makes you feel paralyzed or nervous, or like you are about to hit something. Now relax. Let the sensations of relaxation flood into the muscles of your arms, softening and warming your biceps. Study this delicious feeling of calm relaxation for a moment. (5 sec)

Now turn your attention to your head. Wrinkle your forehead as tightly as you can. Really frown and scowl and make the wrinkles as deep and hard as you can . . . Now relax. Let yourself imagine your entire forehead and scalp becoming as smooth as a baby's forehead. Concentrate on this feeling of smooth relaxation for a moment. (5 sec)

Wrinkle your forehead again. Try to make your whole scalp wrinkly too. Hold it tightly for just a little longer . . . and relax. Let the muscles go, and let your forehead and scalp become as flat as a pool of perfectly still water. Really feel the contrast between a frowning and a relaxed brow. Tell yourself, "I'm letting go of all the tension." (5 sec)

Next, squint your eyes tightly shut. Look for the tension as you keep your eyelids clamped down. Notice how your eyebrows lower and your cheeks go up to pinch your eyes in a vise-grip. Now relax your eyes until they are just barely closed, just very lightly closed, your eyelids just lying softly over your eyes like rose petals. (5 sec)

Close your eyes tightly again. Really clamp them shut like you never intend to open them again. Study the feeling of tension. Then relax your eyes until your lids are just barely lowered. Notice the difference between the tension and the relaxation. Notice whether your eyelids or eyeballs twitch, or feel warm or cool. (5 sec)

Now clench your jaw. Bite down hard, but not hard enough to crack a tooth. Press your teeth firmly together and notice the tension in your jaw. A lot of people grind or press their teeth together unconsciously, creating chronic tension in the jaw muscles. Now relax, letting your mouth open slightly. Feel the release of your jaw muscles as they relax. Let your jaw sag down and study the feeling of relaxation for a moment. (5 sec)

Try it again. Clench your jaw and really concentrate on the feeling of tension. Notice if it reminds you of feeling stubborn or hassled . . . then relax the tension and notice the contrast between muscular tension and relaxed muscles. Let yourself really appreciate the contrast between tension and relaxation. (5 sec)

Now press your tongue against the roof of your mouth. Feel the ache in the back of your mouth and down into your throat . . . Relax your tongue and throat and feel the tension drain out of the muscles. Pay attention to the difference between the tension and the relaxation. (5 sec)

Once more, press your tongue up against the roof of your mouth. Press hard and feel the tension spread from the back of your mouth and down your throat. Study this tension and notice if it reminds you of crying or choking. Now relax the tension and observe the distinctions between tension and relaxation in your throat. (5 sec)

Press your lips forward now, pursing them into an "O." Hold your lips forward in a circle for a while, noticing the tension. Then relax your mouth and let it hang slightly open. Note the difference between the tension and the relaxation for a moment. (5 sec)

Try it again. Push your lips out into the shape of an "O" and hold it, concentrating on the sensations of tension. Then release the muscles and let your mouth relax. Focus on the sensations of calm relaxation. Tell yourself, "I'm allowing tension to flow away." (5 sec)

Next you'll tense and relax the muscles of your neck. A lot of people carry constant tension in their neck muscles. Start by pressing your head back as far as it can comfortably go and observing the tension in your neck. (5 sec)

Now roll your head to the right as far as you can, until you feel strain. Notice the changing location of stress in your muscles. (5 sec)

Then roll your head all the way to the left, as far as you can, and feel how the opposite muscles take up the tension. (5 sec)

Finally, straighten your head and bring it forward, pressing your chin against your chest as far as you can. Notice how this feels for a moment. (5 sec)

Now let your head fall gently back into repose, and relax all the muscles in your neck. Really study the sensations in your neck for another moment. (5 sec)

Repeat this procedure. Press your head back against the floor or bed you're lying on and hold the tension. (5 sec)

Now roll your head to the right and hold it tightly, noticing the tension. (5 sec)

Next roll your head all the way to the left and hold it there. See if the tension feels the same or slightly different from before. (5 sec)

Then raise your head and press your chin towards your chest and hold it up. (5 sec)

Relax, allowing your head to come back to a comfortable position. Study the contrast between the feelings of relaxation and the feelings of contracting and stretching your neck muscles. (5 sec)

Now shrug your shoulders. Keep the tension as you hunch your head down between your shoulders. A lot of tension can also be stored in your shoulders. Hold this pose for a bit, then relax. Allow your shoulders to sag down, and feel the relaxation seeping through your shoulders, neck, and throat. (5 sec)

Shrug your shoulders again. Pull your head down between your shoulders and feel the pressure and tension as you hold the position for a little while. Now relax and let your shoulders go limp. Feel the warmth and heaviness as your shoulders and neck and throat relax. Study the difference in sensation between tension and relaxation. (5 sec)

Give your entire body a chance to relax. Breathe in and fill your lungs completely. Hold your breath and feel the tension in your chest. Now exhale, and let your chest fall and become relaxed. Observe the difference in feeling between tension and relaxation in your chest. (5 sec)

Now inhale again and really fill your lungs to full capacity. Hold the breath and feel the stretching and strain all through your torso. Exhale with a sighing sound and feel relaxation steal over you. Explore the contrasts between the tension of the inhalation and the release of the exhalation. (5 sec)

Next, tighten your stomach muscles and hold them clenched as you focus your attention on the feeling of tension. Then release your stomach muscles, and let the tension subside. Notice how it feels to create tension and then create relaxation. Say to yourself, "I am feeling calmer and more peaceful." (5 sec)

Try tensing your stomach again. Hold the tightness in your stomach and notice if it also makes your lower back feel tight. Relax your stomach muscles and shift your attention to the feelings of relaxation that flow throughout your stomach and lower back. (5 sec)

Now arch your back, without straining. If you have back trouble, skip the tensing part and just imagine draining any tension out of your back muscles. If you are arching your back, focus on the tension in your back muscles. Then relax your back and let it go flat again. This is another area where many people feel chronic muscular tension. Notice how your back feels when it is tense and when it is relaxed. (5 sec)

Now arch your back again. Hold the tension and study it carefully. Does your back feel like this often, when you are not consciously tensing the muscles? Now relax your muscles and let all the strain go away. Observe the contrast between tension and relaxation in your back. (5 sec)

Next, tighten your buttocks and thighs. Flex your thighs by pressing your heels downwards as hard as you can. Hold this tension for a moment, then release it. Feel the relaxation flood into the large muscles of your buttocks and thighs. Concentrate on the subtle differences between tension and relaxation. (5 sec)

Tighten your buttocks and thighs one more time. Push your heels downwards again as hard as you can. Hold this position while you study the tension in your muscles. Now relax, and feel the large muscles relax. Pay attention to the differences between the tense and the loose muscles. (5 sec)

Now curl your toes downwards to make your calf muscles tense. Do this gradually, and stop if you start to get a cramp in the sole of your foot. Hold your toes down, and study the sensation of muscular tension. Then uncurl your toes and release your calf muscles. See if you can perceive all the variations of pressure, stretching, temperature, and slight pain that mark the difference between tension and relaxation. (5 sec)

Try it again. Curl your toes downwards, and tense your calves. Hold the pose while you memorize the feelings of tension. Now relax and feel the sensations of relaxation take over. Try to catalog all the characteristics of relaxation. (5 sec)

Now bend your toes back toward your head, creating tension in your shins. Observe the feeling in your shins as you hold your toes in this position. Now relax and let your toes go back to a comfortable position. Notice the difference between the tension in your shins and the relaxation. (5 sec)

One more time, bend your toes back toward your head and hold the tension in your shins while you analyze the feelings associated with the contracted muscles. Then relax the muscles, let your feet down, and examine the new feeling of relaxation in your shins. Tell yourself, "The tension is melting away." (5 sec)

Lie still for a little while and enjoy the relaxation you have created in your body. You can create relaxation in your body just as naturally as you can create tension in your muscles.

In a moment you will open you eyes and get up. Remind yourself to take time during the next few hours to do your relaxation exercises. Now recall what your surroundings are like, open your eyes slowly, and get up when you are ready. Go about your routine feeling refreshed and relaxed.

Shorthand Procedure

When you have gained some experience in relaxing your body, you may be able to use this shorthand procedure most of the time, instead of the full procedure.

To do the shorthand procedure, curl both your fists and tighten your biceps in a "Charles Atlas" pose. Hold this position, and really concentrate on making your muscles as hard and tight as you can. Then relax, and let your arms fall to your sides. Feel the relaxation rush into the muscles as they go slack.

Next work on your head and neck. Wrinkle up your forehead in a frown, squint your eyes closed, purse your lips, and press your tongue up against the roof of your mouth. Try to wrinkle up your whole face like the shell of a walnut. At the same time, press your head back as far as possible, then roll it around in a complete circle. Reverse and roll your head around in the opposite direction. Then let everything relax, and enjoy the warm feeling of relaxation as your face goes smooth and your neck loosens.

Then arch your back as you take a deep breath into your chest. Hold the breath and tense your stomach muscles. Keep holding the breath and focusing on the feelings of tension. Now flatten your back, exhale, relax the tension in your stomach. Notice how very relaxing it is to breathe out and relax like this.

Finally, tighten your buttocks and thighs. At the same time, curl your toes down to tighten your calves. Hold this position for a moment and concentrate on what tension in your legs feels like. Then relax and switch to analyzing the feelings of relaxation.

Variations. There are other possibilities that you might want to try for altering the basic relaxation procedures. You can start at your feet and work upwards for a little variety. You can try synchronizing your breathing with the tensing and relaxing, so that you breathe in while tensing, hold your breath while holding tension, and then exhale slowly while relaxing your muscles.

As you become more expert at relaxation, you will need less time to tense and relax all your muscles. Also, when you become an expert at noticing muscular tension, the deliberate tensing of your muscles will become less important. You may want to switch to a "body awareness method," in which you systematically scan your body for tension and release it from your muscles without first tensing them. This method is not only faster, it is also preferable if you have sore or injured muscles that you don't want to aggravate with extra tension.

Try different relaxation sequences and methods until you find the ones that give you the best results.

Cleansing Breath

Proper breathing is very important in stress reduction. If your breathing is shallow, with short breaths in a choppy or lazy rhythm, you may not get enough oxygen. Your complexion will be poor because your blood is dark and bluish instead of bright red. Your digestion will be bad, you'll get tired easily, you'll have trouble coping with daily hassles, and you'll tend to fall more easily into states of anxiety and depression. Full, deep, slow breathing corrects these tendencies by relaxing your body, oxygenating your blood, and removing waste from your circulatory system.

Although Westerners have only recently learned about the importance of breathing, Eastern cultures have for centuries used breathing exercises to relax the body and calm the mind.

Here is a script for the cleansing breath exercise, which you may want to tape record for your own use.

> *Lie down, get comfortable, and close your eyes. Put your attention on your breathing. Place your hand on the spot that rises the most when you inhale. If this spot is on your chest, you are not using your full lung capacity. You're breathing mostly in the top of your lungs. Put your hand on your stomach and take full, deep breaths that*

make your stomach rise more than your chest.

Continue breathing slowly and deeply into your stomach. As you inhale, imagine that your nostrils are located in your heels. See your breath as a white cloud of steam or fog, very pure and cleansing. It comes in at your heels and sweeps up the back of your body, reaching your head as your lungs become full. The cloud picks up all impurities, tension, distractions, and fatigue as it passes through you. You can visualize these things as darkness, cinders, dust, or cloudiness.

As you exhale, imagine this white cloud swirling around, down the front of your body, picking up more impurities, and exiting through your toes. As your lungs are emptied, the cloud leaves your body entirely and is dissipated in space. It carries with it all the dark impurities, all the gritty tension, all the dusty fatigue, all the cloudy aches and pains.

Keep breathing slowly and deeply. Again, imagine the white cloud coming in at your heels, swirling around to fill every limb and digit, and carrying all the darkness out your toes. Your body gets brighter, cleaner, lighter with each breath.

If the traditional heel and toe imagery doesn't feel comfortable to you, change the entry and exit points to suit yourself. You could have your breath coming in your head and going out your feet, or in your nose and out your mouth, or whatever. Find the arrangement that feels the most logical and cleansing to you.

Cue-Controlled Relaxation

This is a combination of muscle scanning and breathing that allows you to relax very quickly, in two or three minutes. It's the recommended relaxation method for anger control or any other situation in which you need to calm down quickly. The steps are simple:

1. Sit down and close your eyes. Scan your body from your forehead all the way down to your toes. Consciously relax any tight muscles you find. Let relaxation flood your body from head to toe.

   To master this "release only" method of body scanning, you may need to go back and practice progressive muscle relaxation some more, until you have fine-tuned your ability to distinguish between tense and relaxed muscles. In time, this scanning will take just a few seconds.

2. Shift your focus to your breathing, and breathe deeply and slowly. With each inhale, say to yourself, "Breathe in." With each exhale, say to yourself, "Relax." Whatever distractions come to mind, return to these words: "Breathe in . . . Relax . . . Breathe in . . . Relax . . ." Feel each breath bring peace and calm in, and then send anger and worry out.

Visualization

In the cleansing breath exercise you used images of a white cloud and dust to enhance the relaxing effects of deep breathing. In this visualization exercise, you will explore your own personal imagery of tension and relaxation. You'll also work with your other senses—hearing, taste, smell, touch, and so on. This will help you create a vivid constellation of symbols for both tension and relaxation.

To do the visualization exercise, lie down, get comfortable, and let your mind go blank and quiet. Gradually become aware of a spot in your body where you normally feel soreness or tension. It might be your back, your neck, your shoulders, or your jaw.

If that part isn't sore or tense right now, deliberately tense it a little. While you are feeling that muscular tension, what images come up for you? What does your tension look like? What object or experience does it remind you of? What color is it? If you could listen to your tension, what would it sound like? Think of an unpleasant smell that could represent your tension. Is your tension hot or cold? Rough or smooth? Bitter or sour or salty?

Ideally, you should get at least one impression from each of your senses to represent tension: sight, hearing, taste, smell, and the various senses of touch. For example, a medical doctor associated muscular tension with twisted and knotted white cotton sheets, the color blue-green, steel-toed work shoes, resounding Chinese gongs, a high whistling sound, a metallic taste like tinfoil on silver dental fillings, the smell of ether, the feel of a wire brush, and cold wind on wet skin.

You may not get so many impressions. That's okay. The important thing is to get a few images or sensations that you associate strongly with muscular tension in your body.

It's even all right if you come up with no original images at all. You can choose a few from this list:

- Tight, twisted ropes

- Hard, cold wax

- The sound of jackhammers

- Creaking hinges

- The taste of lemon

- The smell of hot metal

- The feel of sandpaper

- Cold wind

- Hot, red muscles

Next, let the tension fade from your muscles. Concentrate on feeling warm, heavy, and completely relaxed. What images come to mind to represent total relaxation? They may be logical extensions or transformations of your images of tension, or they may be new, unrelated images.

For example, the doctor saw the twisted sheets untwisting and becoming soft and smooth. The blue-green color faded to a pale, peachy yellow. The work shoes changed into fleecy bedroom slippers. The Chinese gong modulated into a soft piano sonata. The whistling sound faded into silence. The metallic taste and the smell of ether were replaced by the taste and smell of jasmine tea. The feel of the cold wind went away, to be replaced by warm sand

and sun on the skin. He also associated relaxation with a picture he had once seen of lions sleeping, the sound of distant calliope music, and the sensations of getting a massage.

Once again, if you don't get any spontaneous sensations to represent relaxation, you can choose some from this list:

- Twisted ropes untwist

- Wax softens and melts

- Jackhammers become distant woodpeckers

- Hinges get oiled and become silent and smooth

- The taste of lemon becomes your favorite dessert

- The smell of hot metal becomes the smell of roses

- Sandpaper becomes silk

- Cold wind becomes warm sun

- Hot, red muscles turn a cool green color

The images you choose for your first stress reduction visualizations are not too crucial. As you practice, you will be attracted to the right images for you, and new images will present themselves as you develop your skills.

When you want to work on relaxing a particular part of your body, first imagine your symbol for tension, then locate it in the area of your body you want to concentrate on. For example, if you have chronic lower back pain, imagine that there are ropes in your lower back. They are twisted so tight that they are quivering with tension. Imagine the finest details: the color of the rope, the number of strands in each, the texture, the play of light and shadow over the ropes. Then bring in your personal symbol for relaxation. Imagine the ropes slackening. Watch them untwist. Feel them loosen their grip on your spine. See the ropes finally go limp and hang free, with no tension left at all.

Example

Karen was under a lot of stress. Her driver's license had been suspended because of a DUI arrest. She had to commute nearly two hours on the bus to her job. In her drinking days she had missed so much work that she was still under a cloud there, and couldn't afford to miss even an hour. She was going to three AA meetings a week, and felt like she was barely hanging on to her sobriety. Her dad was in the hospital, dying of emphysema. Her son Jason was awaiting trial on drug charges, and she was afraid he would jump bail and skip town.

Karen had always had a bad stomach. Years of drinking had made her ulcers worse, and she had irritable bowel syndrome, with recurring pain in her intestines. She ground her teeth in her sleep, and had chronic jaw pain.

She got started with relaxation exercises at the suggestion of the pharmacist who originally recommended *Tagamet* for ulcer pain. She practiced progressive muscle relaxation before she went to bed each night. After a few nights, she could get herself relaxed enough to sleep more peacefully, with less teeth grinding. She started doing the shorthand technique on the bus on her way home, so that she arrived home from work more relaxed and ready to cope with her message machine and her evening trips to the hospital to visit her dad or go to AA meetings.

At work, Karen took coffee breaks in the women's room, sitting in a locked stall and doing deep breathing. She took several breaths to calm herself before important meetings or phone calls. She found that sitting up straighter at her desk made it easier to breathe and reduced her intestinal cramps.

Karen visualized her ulcers as hot coals. When she did her relaxation exercises, she imagined ice water seeping into her stomach and extinguishing the coals. She envisioned her intestinal cramps as twisted dishtowels, wound up so tight that they formed hard knots and kinks. She imagined the water seeping into the towels, making them untwist and relax. The towels changed to warm compresses, soothing her.

Relaxation wasn't the total answer to Karen's problems, but it helped her cope during a very stressful time in her life. Learning to relax on command helped her get through her license suspension, her dad's funeral, her son's trial, and an anxious period of down-sizing at work—without relapsing

8

Feelings

In recovery circles you hear about "dry drunks"—people who have stopped drinking and drugging, but are still angry, irritable, depressed, fearful, nervous, confused, and unhappy. The term dry drunk is often used in a critical sense as a put-down.

Actually, painful emotions such as anxiety, anger, and depression are part of the normal withdrawal syndrome that you can expect to feel for some time after you stop consuming powerful drugs like alcohol or cocaine. It's normal and reasonable to feel depressed, and to mourn the loss of your chemically dependent lifestyle. It's normal and reasonable to feel angry about other people's ability to drink or use drugs in moderation without the loss of control that drove you to sobriety. It's normal and reasonable to feel guilt, remorse, and shame about excesses committed under the influence. It's normal and reasonable to feel scared about your ability to stay sober and deal with your life without alcohol or drugs.

But what do you do when bad feelings persist for months and months? What do you do when your feelings don't feel normal or reasonable, when they obviously aren't temporary withdrawal symptoms but chronic psychological problems?

This chapter will help you recognize your chronic negative emotions, express them appropriately, analyze them, and develop the skills you need to relieve them.

You may find that this chapter alone is enough to ease bad feelings. Or you may decide to get additional help from an addiction counselor, psychologist, social worker, or other helping professional. *You should definitely seek outside help if any of the following are true for you:*

- Your anger is so out of control that you are striking out at other people

- Your fears are keeping you isolated at home

- Your depression has inspired thoughts of suicide

- Your feelings are destroying important relationships

Identifying and Expressing Your Feelings

Sometimes chemically dependent people are out of touch with their feelings. If this is the case for you, this section will give you exercises for discovering what you feel, and expressing it to others.

Some chemically dependent people are extremely aware of their feelings, to the point of being overwhelmed or carried away by them. They need help in controlling and coping with feelings, not in identifying and expressing them. Still others may repress feelings, stuffing them down until they finally squirt out in undesirable ways. If you are paying a price for a lack of emotional management skills, you should go on to the sections about analyzing and changing your feelings.

Identifying Your Feelings

In the space below, briefly describe a situation that has been bothering you. It can be a relationship with someone close, a work situation, a persistent memory, a confusing exchange you had with someone—any situation in which you have had confused feelings.

Problem situation: _____

_____

_____

Now choose one the following observations about the problem:

☐ *Feels Good*   ☐ *Feels Bad*

This is the starting point. Just answer one or the other, depending on whether the situation felt mostly good or mostly bad. If you're not positive, go with your hunch.

All emotions are associated with physical sensations such as tightness in the chest, racing pulse, fatigue, sweating, butterflies in the stomach, and so on. Close your eyes, focus on your breathing, and imagine that you are back in the situation. Keep remembering the situation until you can feel the good or bad feeling. Scan your body and see where the feeling seems to reside: mostly in your chest, your stomach, your hands, your head?

Location in your body: _____

Concentrating on the area most closely associated with the feeling, ask yourself how much space it takes up. Is it large or small? If you could fill up the area with water, how much would it hold—a pint? A quart? A gallon?

"Size": _____

When you have an idea of the size, try to sense a shape. Trace the feeling's boundaries, and determine whether it's round, square, jagged, oval, or whatever.

"Shape": _____

Now write down the color that comes to mind when you contemplate the feeling. Is it warm, like orange or red? Is it cool, like blue or green?

"Color": _____

If you can't get any clear ideas about location, size, shape, and so on, don't pass judgment on yourself. Just guess. Put down any place or size or shape. You can come back later and alter your answers when the feeling becomes clearer.

Now imagine that your feeling can talk. What would it say if it could talk by itself? Put down anything that comes to mind, even if it doesn't make sense. It could be a word like *loss* or *strange* or *bad*. It could be a phrase or a sentence that makes sense or doesn't make sense. Or you may hear only silence, or see an image or hear a sound. Again, don't pass judgment on yourself. Just write whatever comes to mind.

What it says to you: _____

_____

_____

What does the feeling make you want to do? Run? Hug someone? Hit someone? Hide? Cry? Let your imagination go, and see yourself doing whatever the feeling calls for. This is fantasy, not real life, so you can indulge yourself in something that you wouldn't actually do, like hitting, spitting, calling names, and so on.

What it makes you want to do: _____

_____

_____

When have you had this kind of feeling before? What was going on? Who was there? Were you able to identify the feeling then? Did you express it? How? Do these situations come up frequently, forming a pattern for you? For instance, do you habitually retreat from intimacy? Do you tend to get sexually involved too soon or too often? Do you have chronic trouble with authority figures? Have you always handled frustration poorly?

Similar Past Situations: _____

_____

_____

By now you should be able to give your feeling a name or several names. The words may not be an exact match to what you feel, but they should be close. To help, here is a list of common feelings. Scan it to improve your feeling vocabulary.

List of Words You Can Use To Describe a Given Feeling

Affectionate	Glad	Relaxed
Afraid	Gloomy	Relieved
Amused	Grateful	Resentful
Angry	Great	Resigned
Annoyed	Guilty	Sad
Anxious	Happy	Safe
Apathetic	Hateful	Satisfied
Apprehensive	Helpless	Secure
Ashamed	Hopeless	Sexy
Bitter	Horrified	Shy
Bored	Hostile	Silly
Calm	Impatient	Strong
Capable	Inadequate	Stubborn
Cheerful	Inhibited	Stuck
Comfortable	Irritated	Supportive
Competent	Isolated	Sympathetic
Concerned	Jealous	Tearful
Confident	Joyful	Tender
Confused	Lonely	Terrified
Contemptuous	Loved	Threatened
Controlled	Loving	Thrilled
Curious	Loyal	Touchy
Defeated	Manipulated	Trapped
Dejected	Manipulative	Troubled
Delighted	Melancholy	Unappreciated
Depressed	Miserable	Uncertain
Desirable	Misunderstood	Understood
Despairing	Muddled	Uneasy
Desperate	Needy	Unfulfilled
Determined	Nervous	Unimportant
Devastated	Numb	Unloved
Disappointed	Out of control	Upset
Discouraged	Outraged	Uptight
Disgusted	Overwhelmed	Used
Disillusioned	Panicky	Useless
Distrustful	Passionate	Victimized
Embarrassed	Peaceful	Violated
Enraged	Pessimistic	Vulnerable
Exasperated	Playful	Withdrawn
Excited	Pleased	Wonderful
Frantic	Powerful	Worn out
Frightened	Prejudiced	Worried
Frustrated	Pressured	Worthless
Fulfilled	Proud	Worthwhile
Furious	Provoked	Wronged
Generous	Put down	Yearning

Now give a name to your feeling.

Best word to describe this feeling: _____

During the time when Derek was trying to stop drinking and smoking dope, he felt very uncomfortable whenever his girlfriend Janine pressured him about moving in with her. But he could never explain his feelings to her. After doing this exercise, he determined that his feeling was a bad one, centered in his stomach, about the size and shape and color of a football. If it had a voice, the feeling would have said, "Leave me alone!" It made him want to escape. Specifically, he wanted to go off by himself and smoke a joint—which certainly didn't help him in his efforts to quit smoking marijuana. The feeling reminded him of the time a few years earlier, when his dad and the high school counselor were trying to get Derek to apply to college, when all he wanted to do was play music and work in a music store.

Derek was able to name his feelings as *pressured, anxious,* and *afraid*—afraid of commitment, and simultaneously afraid to say no. Doing this exercise allowed him to talk to Janine about these feelings for the first time. Eventually Derek was able to see that he was afraid of commitment because he was terrified of failure. If he moved in with Janine and it didn't work out, it would represent failure. If he tried college, he might fail. If he stopped drinking and smoking, then relapsed, he would have to face yet another failure. On the other hand, if he successfully quit alcohol and drugs, he'd have fewer excuses for not getting on with his life. His feelings were ambivalent and painful—but at least now he was able to know what they were.

Keeping a Feelings Diary. Carry a card or notebook around with you, and practice identifying your feelings. Use these guidelines for characterizing each feeling.

Situation: _____

☐ *Feels Good*   ☐ *Feels Bad*

Location in your body: _____

"Size": _____

"Shape": _____

"Color": _____

What it says to you: _____

What it makes you want to do: _____

Similar past situations: _____

Best word to describe this feeling: _____

Expressing Your Feelings

This exercise will give you a framework for expressing feelings, starting with a key feeling word and modifying it. Do this exercise on paper before trying to express a difficult feeling to someone. Later, the process will become more familiar, and you will be able to express your feelings spontaneously.

Use the list of feeling words given earlier, and write down the single word that best describes how you feel.

Key feeling word: _____

Clarify the key word by explaining what it means to you. For example, "upset" might mean worried and concerned to one person, but angry and disappointed to someone else. Define your term.

What this feeling means to me: _____

Use modifying words like *a little, very, really* to describe the intensity of your feeling. If you're angry, say "I'm a little angry," or "I'm really angry with you." Use more precise adjectives to clarify the intensity of your feeling: "I'm irritated and annoyed," or "I'm furious—I'm enraged."

Intensity: _____

Identify how long the feeling has been going on. "All this month," or "This morning," or "Ever since our honeymoon."

Duration: _____

It's tempting to attribute your feelings to what someone else did or said. But as logical as it may seem that your feelings are simply a reaction, this way of looking at them actually robs you of a sense of independence and control. When you say to someone, "You make me feel crazy," you're making that person responsible for your feelings; in other words, you're blaming them for how you feel. This is guaranteed to alienate the person you're talking to. It's also simply untrue. No one *makes* anyone else feel something. Feelings originate inside of us. As inevitable as a feeling might seem—fear or grief, for instance—it's important to realize that you choose to feel what you feel, on a certain level. Feelings are not like reflexes: they're subject to adjustment and fine-tuning. Taking responsibility for your feelings allows you to "own" them—so that you can actually do something about them.

In the space below, describe the *context* of your feelings, rather than implying that someone else caused you to feel this way. Using "I" rather than "You" to begin your sentences will greatly help this process. For example, don't say, "You made me mad." Rather, give your feelings a context by saying, "I felt mad after you left last night." This may seem a subtle distinction, but it will make all the difference in the world in terms of how you're heard, and how in control you feel.

Cause and Context: _____

_____

If it's applicable, mention when you have felt this way before.

Historical Precedents: _____

Here's how Wilma, a 53-year-old woman just coming out of an in-patient detox program, expressed her feelings to her husband:

I felt angry (*key feeling word*) when you and the kids told me I had to go to the center (*context*). I felt manipulated and ganged-up-on (*definition*). For a whole week, I alternated between rage and despair (*intensity and duration*). It was like the time when Susie and James didn't invite me to the christening, only worse (*historical precedent*). I hate it when anybody tells me what to do (*more context*).

Analyzing Your Feelings

In the space below, describe a situation that has made you feel bad in the past. It can be a situation in which you ended up drinking or taking drugs, or any other situation involving strong feelings. Use extra paper if you want to.

Situation	Feeling

Here are a couple of examples:

Situation	Feeling
Nancy asks me to go to a party given by people she works with	Manipulated Reluctant
Daughter spills milk all over dinner table after I've told her to stop goofing off	Enraged Frustrated

That's all you have to do at this point. You'll come back to this situation and feeling several times later on in this workbook. But right now you need to consider how feelings are created. There are two main theories to account for where feelings come from, and how to control them.

The Pressure Tank Theory of Feelings

When you were a kid, did you ever play with vinegar and baking soda? The acid in the vinegar makes the baking soda bubble and foam, releasing a lot of gas. The "Pressure

Tank" theory of feelings assumes that your emotional responses to life resemble this kind of chemical reaction. According to this commonly held theory, when the vinegar of daily experience hits the baking soda of your psyche, emotions are formed like rapidly expanding clouds of gas. The emotions are contained somehow within you, like propane in a pressure tank, until you either:

- Vent your feelings in some appropriate way

- Lose control, and your feelings explode outward (anger)

- Or succumb to the pressure and implode inward (depression)

The pressure tank theory is popular. It seems intuitively correct, since it describes what emotions such as anger feel like when you're trying to control them. But there are three problems with the theory. First, the pressure tank theory doesn't explain why you sometimes get irritated at your noisy kids, while sometimes you don't. If emotions were really like vinegar and soda, you would get a constant reaction every time the same situation came up.

Second, the pressure tank theory doesn't account for the fact that the mere *thought* of your job can make you feel depressed, even if you are not at work at the time. There must be some connection between feelings and thoughts that the pressure tank theory doesn't take into consideration.

The third problem with the pressure tank theory is its implicit suggestion that the way to handle your feelings is to express them—to let off steam before too much dangerous pressure builds up. This is applied most often to anger: "You've got to vent your anger, not bottle it up inside you until it explodes inappropriately." However, psychologists who study anger have found this folk wisdom to be completely wrong. People who frequently vent their anger tend to get *angrier* as time goes by.

The Generator Theory of Feelings

These drawbacks to the pressure tank theory have led cognitive psychologists such as Aaron Beck to propose the "Generator" theory of feelings. According to this theory, feelings are created by your mind, in a way similar to that in which electricity is created by a generator.

Here's how it works. Your mind is constantly thinking thoughts about what's going on in the present, about the past, and about the future. These thoughts spin around in your mind with the effect of a generator making electricity. Your body is wired to your mind like colored lights wired to a generator. Certain thoughts light up the red anger light. Other thoughts light up the blue depression light, or the green pleasure light, or the yellow fear light, and so on.

The generator theory solves the three problems of the pressure tank theory. First, it explains why sometimes you get irritated at those noisy kids and sometimes you don't. One time your thought is, "Those brats are out of control"—and that lights up your annoyance. Another time, the thought is, "Look at them, full of energy and life"—and that lights up a feeling of pride or appreciation.

Secondly, the generator theory explains perfectly why you don't have to be at work to feel depressed about your job. All emotions such as depression start as thoughts. It isn't being at work itself that depresses you—it's thoughts such as, "I hate my job" or "Tomorrow's Monday and I have to go to work," or "I'm stuck here until five." You get depressed whenever you have the depressing thoughts, whether you're at work or not.

Third, the generator theory suggests a way of getting control over your feelings that really works: you can change your feelings by changing your thoughts.

Cognitive Therapy

That's the essence of cognitive therapy: Change the way you feel by changing your thoughts. This chapter will teach several cognitive therapy methods for uncovering the thoughts that make you feel bad, and changing them to more positive thoughts.

Cognitive techniques have several advantages for chemically dependent people:

- You can relieve the negative feelings that make you prone to relapse.

- You can reduce cravings by modifying the automatic thoughts that power your urges to drink or use drugs.

- You can increase your willpower by composing affirmative coping thoughts and reciting them to yourself.

- You can develop and practice new patterns of thought that reinforce long-term life-style changes.

Your Inner Voice

If you're quiet and listen to your own mind, you'll hear your inner voice. Most people's thoughts seem to them like a voice inside them, constantly commenting on the passing scene, telling stories about the past, predicting the future, passing judgments on self and others, explaining and interpreting, wishing and wanting. Sometimes the voice is accompanied by images. You might say to yourself, "I miss Jennie," and in your mind's eye you'll see an image of your sister Jennie waving goodbye.

Your inner voice is like a radio or TV playing in the background. It's always on, so most of the time you're not very aware of it. You are more aware of the feelings that the thoughts generate: boredom, restlessness, sadness, anxiety, pleasure, irritation.

For example, when you feel nervous before a blind date, it's because your inner voice is saying things like, "I'll make a fool or myself," or "I'm too fat."

The Addictive Inner Voice

If you're chemically dependent, you have an addictive inner voice. In AA they call it "Stinkin' Thinkin'." In Rational Recovery groups they talk about the "beast" that whispers in your ear. They're all talking about the addictive inner voice that makes you feel frustrated or bored or restless, and convinces you to take a drink or do a line. The voice causes those feelings by saying things like, "There's nothing to do here, this is a drag, I can't stand it. Let's have a little taste."

Addictive thoughts commonly take several forms:

1. Deep core beliefs about yourself

I'm no good.

I'm a failure.

I'm trapped.

The world is against me.

I must succeed at all costs.

Nobody loves me.

I'm a misfit, an outsider.

I'm too damaged to recover.

2. Pleasure-seeking thoughts

It'll be fun.

Let's party.

You only live once.

3. Problem-solving thoughts

I'll be more social if I drink.

I'm more creative when I'm tipsy.

It will give me energy.

4. Stress-relieving thoughts

Just one beer to calm the shakes.

It numbs the pain of my arthritis.

It's my only release from a lousy marriage.

5. Permission-giving beliefs

I deserve it.

Well, I'm drunk now—might as well get drunker.

Just this once, then back on the wagon.

Here are the examples given previously, with thoughts added. Notice how they make more sense with the cognitive link between what happens and what you feel:

Situation	Thoughts	Feeling
Nancy asks me to go to a party given by people she works with	I'll feel bored and shy. I'll want a drink. If I do drink, I'll hate myself. Why does Nancy set me up like this?	Manipulated Reluctant
Daughter spills milk all over dinner table after I've told her to stop goofing off	She's doing it on purpose to annoy me. I saw what she did—she looked at me first before she knocked it over.	Frustrated Enraged

Exercise

Use the same situation and feeling you used earlier in the chapter, but add a column for your thoughts:

Situation	Thoughts	Feeling
_____	_____	_____
_____	_____	_____
_____	_____	_____
_____	_____	_____
_____	_____	_____
_____	_____	_____
_____	_____	_____
_____	_____	_____
_____	_____	_____

Remember the Denial Checklist from the chapter called "Do You Have a Problem?" And the Decision Box in "Getting Ready to Quit," in which you listed the good things about continuing to drink or take drugs and the bad things about quitting? The statements and reasons you listed in those exercises are good examples of the thoughts that make up your addictive inner voice. You can go back to those exercises to get hints about your negative addictive thoughts.

Changing Your Feelings by Changing Negative Thoughts

Positive thoughts lead to positive feelings, just as negative thoughts lead to negative feelings. If you tell yourself, "He likes her more than he likes me," you're bound to feel disappointment and jealousy. If you tell yourself instead, "He'll like me when he gets to know me," you'll tend to feel less jealousy, and a greater sense of confidence and positive anticipation.

Here's how the previous examples look when completed with positive thoughts and feelings:

Situation	Negative Thoughts	Negative Feelings (% intensity)	Positive Thoughts	More Positive Feelings/ (% intensity)
Nancy asks me to go to a party given by people she works with.	I'll feel bored and shy. I'll want a drink. If I do drink, I'll hate myself. Why does Nancy set me up like this?	Manipulated 90% Reluctant 100%	Nancy wants me to get to know the people she works with everyday. She obviously thinks I can cope. I can talk to her about my misgivings before I make a decision whether to go.	More empowered 50% More willing to consider going 50%
Daughter spills milk all over dinner table after I've told her to stop goofing off.	She's doing it on purpose to annoy me. I saw what she did. She looked at me first before she knocked it over.	Enraged 99% Frustrated	She has very few options at her age for controlling her environment. She wanted my attention, and I was busy talking to Tim. Things will get easier when she's more confident and articulate.	Exasperated but resigned. Feeling of empathy 30%

Notice that the negative feelings are now rated by percentage of intensity, using a 1-100 scale. The more positive feelings are also rated to show how the intensity of the bad feelings has declined. Often a situation doesn't lend itself to a purely positive feeling. Instead, the positive thoughts serve to reduce the severity of the negative feelings to a level where they are tolerable.

To practice identifying the thought-feeling connection, match up this list of thoughts and feelings. Connect each item in the first column by a line leading to an item in the other three columns.

Negative Thought	Negative Feeling	Alternate Positive Thought	More Positive Feeling
I'm all alone	Angry	*I'm doing the best I can*	Lonely but hopeful
I've done wrong	Depressed	*He's just trying to protect himself*	More confident
He's horrible	Shy	*I can meet someone new now that I'm clean and sober.*	Less guilty, dignity intact
They'll reject me	Guilty	*I can take care of myself; I don't require approval.*	Irritated but accepting

How did you do? Check your answers against this key:

Negative Thought	Negative Feeling	Alternate Positive Thought	More Positive Feeling
I'm all alone	Angry	*I'm doing the best I can*	Lonely but hopeful
I've done wrong	Depressed	*He's just trying to protect himself*	More confident
He's horrible	Shy	*I can meet someone new now that I'm clean and sober.*	Less guilty, dignity intact
They'll reject me	Guilty	*I can take care of myself; I don't require approval.*	Irritated but accepting

Add positive thoughts and feelings to the situation you have been working on in this chapter. Use extra paper if you need it.

Situation	Negative Thoughts	Negative Feelings (% intensity)	Positive Thoughts	Positive Feelings (% intensity)
_____	_____	_____	_____	_____
_____	_____	_____	_____	_____
_____	_____	_____	_____	_____
_____	_____	_____	_____	_____

Thoughts and Feelings Diary

By now you have enough practice recording your thoughts and feelings to keep a daily diary. Carry a small card or notebook around with you. Whenever you feel upset, depressed, bored, anxious, or whatever, take a moment to record the situation, your thoughts, and the feelings you're experiencing. Or make photocopies of this page, and carry one copy around with you. Use the five-column format.

If you can't write things down at the moment, spend a few minutes before bed each night catching up on your diary. Include the last two columns—positive thoughts and feelings—even if you didn't think any positive thoughts during the actual events. This will give you good practice in making up refutations of your negative takes on yourself and others.

Situation	Negative Thoughts	Negative Feelings (% intensity)	Positive Thoughts	More Positive Feelings (% intensity)
_____	_____	_____	_____	_____
_____	_____	_____	_____	_____
_____	_____	_____	_____	_____
_____	_____	_____	_____	_____
_____	_____	_____	_____	_____
_____	_____	_____	_____	_____
_____	_____	_____	_____	_____
_____	_____	_____	_____	_____
_____	_____	_____	_____	_____
_____	_____	_____	_____	_____
_____	_____	_____	_____	_____
_____	_____	_____	_____	_____
_____	_____	_____	_____	_____

Example

Esther was an alcoholic who had been sober for six months. At her AA meetings they called her a classic "dry drunk." She was often irritable and short-tempered with her twenty-two-year-old daughter, who lived with her. Esther argued with people over minor matters. She was often depressed by her failure to find a new job after she got fired from her job managing a trailer park. She felt anxious every time she thought about going out to interview for a new job.

Esther resolved to ease her painful emotions by changing her "stinkin' thinkin'." She kept a thoughts and feelings diary for three weeks. Here are some entries she made:

Situation	Negative Thoughts	Negative Feelings (% intensity)	Positive Thoughts	More Positive Feelings (% intensity)
Donna leaves pizza box and Coke cans all over living room	She's such a slob; she just makes things harder for me. It's time she started giving something back.	Resentful, Critical 75%	Donna and I could do a spring cleaning together. If she gets a little invested in how this place looks, she might start developing some better habits.	Resigned, Excited 25%
Cashing last unemployment check	I'll be broke in less than two weeks. I'm a failure. I'm doomed.	Depressed 100%	I worked 28 years, I'll work again.	Guarded faith, optimism 10%
Calling for job interview	They'll hate me. I'm too old. They'll read my history in my face.	Anxious, Panicky 30%	I had the strength to get sober. I can handle a job interview.	Self-respect, self-confidence 85%

Often Esther got only a hint of one word or a dim image when she first tried to observe her negative thoughts. She had to lie on her couch and relive a painful experience in slow motion in her imagination several times before the negative thoughts were clear enough for her to write them down.

Esther realized that many of the AA sayings that she had previously referred to as "bumper sticker therapy" were in fact very good positive thoughts that fit right in with her personal program of cognitive therapy. When she felt moved to criticize her daughter, she'd tell herself, "Live and let live." When she began to obsess about the future and her financial problems, she would remind herself to live "one day at a time," and "stay in the now." When she got angry at someone in the program, she'd remember to "drop the rock" and work on an attitude of "reliance, not defiance." When she went to a job interview with the owner of some laundromats, she "acted as if" she were a mature, well-balanced person who could handle problems calmly.

Esther wrote some of her best positive affirmations on a stick-on note and put it inside the cellophane on her pack of cigarettes. Every time she lit up, she read one of the affirmations to remind her of her new positive thoughts.

Every time she opened her refrigerator, she saw a bookmark bearing the Serenity Prayer magneted to the door:

> *"God grant me:*
> *the serenity to accept the things I cannot change,*
> *the courage to change the things I can,*
> *and the wisdom to know the difference."*

Esther eventually got the job managing a string of three laundromats. Her daughter moved out to her own apartment. Their relationship improved because of Esther's improved emotional equilibrium, and because she and Donna weren't living together in a small mobile home. Esther made a new friend in the AA program, and celebrated her first anniversary of sobriety by telling her story at a meeting.

As her painful emotions subsided and came more under her control, Esther regained access to some loving, caring, nurturing feelings that she remembered having toward her pets when she was a girl, and toward Donna when she was an infant. Esther began offering support to others in AA, adopted a cat at the SPCA, and got some house plants for her trailer.

Special Considerations

Depression—Should You Medicate?

If you're depressed and under a physician's care these days, you will probably be advised to take an anti-depressant medication such as *Prozac.*

Some conservative addiction counselors and old-line AA members will tell you not to take any kind of mood-altering drug, since your whole problem revolves around dependence on mood-altering chemicals. This attitude arises partly from common sense, partly from a moral judgment, and partly from people's memory of a time when alcoholics and addicts were given tranquilizers and other powerful psychoactive drugs that merely substituted one addiction for another.

The new drugs for depression are very effective, are not addictive, and have few long-term side effects for most people. They do not produce euphoria or dramatic alterations of consciousness. What they do is simply normalize. The strongest proof that these medications are not addictive is that many recovering people report forgetting to take them as prescribed. They never forgot to take their drug of choice. If you are advised to take one of these newer medications, you should seriously consider doing so, at least for a trial period. It is much more likely to promote your sobriety than impede it.

Long-term Work With Feelings

This chapter is designed to help you cope with painful feelings in the short term, during your first year or so of being clean and sober. There's lots more you can do in the long term.

Adult children of alcoholics and addicts have common patterns of thoughts, feelings, and behaviors that have been explained and explored fully by the ACoA movement. There are many excellent books and groups that can help you deal with these issues as you progress in your recovery. Look in the addiction section of a good bookstore for titles on codependence and inner child work.

9

Spirituality

Over and over in books, at AA meetings, and among recovering alcoholics and addicts you will hear that addiction is a "spiritual" problem.

What does this mean?

Does it mean that addiction can only be cured by joining a religion? By praying to God as you understand Him/Her? By obeying the ten commandments? By doing penance for past sins?

Not exactly. Your spiritual path out of addiction may at some point lead you through organized religion and conventional morality. But the spiritual nature of addiction and recovery is grounded in the individual, in your attempts to answer these timeless questions:

Who am I?
Where is my place in the universe?
What is the meaning of life?
What is worth doing?
Do I have free will?
Can I love and be loved?
How can I know what's true?
Why is there pain and death?

For some people who are chemically dependent, the answers to these questions tend to have a defiant, grandiose tone, and may sound like this:

I'm the center of the universe. It all revolves around me. Life has no special meaning
beyond my own desires. Nothing's really worth doing, so I might as well have fun.
I have no free will to speak of—but if I take another drink, I'll at least feel free for
a while. I can do whatever I want. Nobody loves me, but who needs 'em? It's

impossible to figure out what's true, so why not roll another joint, do another line? Life is short, then you die. I'm going to grab for all the gusto I can get while I'm alive.

Or, if you tend more toward depression than rage, your answers might lean more toward the tragic and hopeless:

I'm nobody. There's no place where I really belong. Life is meaningless, and I can't do anything about it—so why not drown my sorrows? I'm trapped in a dead-end universe with no hope, no freedom, no chance of love; so it doesn't matter what I put inside me to ease the pain.

This is the spiritual theme music of addiction that underscores its moods of guilt, shame, rage, terror, and misery. These spiritually deadening messages rumble along in your subconscious like minor-key subsonics in a movie soundtrack, which make every day seem like you're dodging across a battlefield or slogging through a swamp.

When you begin to emerge out of the darkness of dependence into the light of sobriety, you may start to wake up and hear this music. You look for ways to refute the grandiose or depressing messages and replace them with hope. Your straight, sober answers to the important spiritual questions begin to assert themselves:

I'm not the center of the universe, but I'm somebody; I matter. I have a proper place in the scheme of things. I can discover the meaning of life for myself, find out what I really want to do. I can be free of chemicals and the past. I am capable of loving and being loved. I can stay clean and sober, and face the truth of reality. Life is too short and precious to risk losing my clear-headed experience of it to the influence of some chemical.

The theme music of recovery is in a major key. The actual notes that make up the melody are your own to arrange. The spiritual work of recovery is an ongoing process of discovering your own music of the spheres. Every day you play out another chorus as you ask yourself, "What is my stance toward the universe? Toward others? Toward alcohol and drugs? Will I remain free today, or become enslaved again?"

Is this just a fancy metaphor, a pep-talk in the language of New Age spirituality? Not entirely. A scientific study (Waisberg, 1994) gave 131 adult alcoholics a "Purpose in Life" test before and after treatment. Before they dealt with their alcoholism, most of the subjects scored way below the average—they saw little purpose in their lives. After treatment, most scored within the average range for a sense of life purpose.

The following exercises are designed to encourage your spiritual exploration and growth. Do them. They will put you in a spiritual frame of mind, situate you in the right place at the right time for positive change, and point you in the right direction. Where you go from there is up to you. You may perform the steps of an exercise and find that nothing happens. You may get precisely the results we predict. Or you may go off on a tangent, and reach spiritual realms we never dreamed of. Regardless of your results, take what you get without judgment. There is no way to make a mistake in this chapter, except by not trying at all.

Warmups

Stream-of-Consciousness Writing

Write for ten minutes, without thinking or editing or erasing or crossing out. Try not even looking at the page directly. Try to get words to flow from your mind straight on the paper, without going through your conscious mind at all. If you find yourself too self-critical, you might try writing left-handed if you are right handed, and vice versa (if you can); or typing at a computer or a word processor. Don't judge. It doesn't matter if you misspell or write in unconnected phrases. What you write doesn't have to make sense. You can jump around from one topic to another. Don't think of showing this to anybody. If you have trouble getting started, try writing a description of the room you're in, or use one of these phrases as a jumping-off point:

When I was small, my mother _____

The trouble with alcohol/drugs is _____

If I could change one thing in life _____

Right now, I feel _____

The most beautiful thing I ever saw was _____

I'm worried about _____

I'm angry about _____

I'm sad about _____

I feel so guilty about _____

I'm jealous of _____

I'm afraid of _____

I resent _____

Observing Nature

Take a walk outdoors. It can be in your backyard, a field, a park—anywhere. Find someplace where you can observe things growing. Sit down on the ground and look at whatever is right in front of you. Notice the colors and textures, the plants growing, and the bits of dead plant matter. Catalog the litter. Review what you know about plants growing, dying, decaying, feeding new generations of plants. Remind yourself that this natural cycle goes on and on, and will continue to go on, whether you exist to observe it or not.

Soon, human nature being what it is, you will be thrown back to thoughts of yourself. Think of how you are also part of nature—an animal that has its own niche in the natural world, and needs to breathe, drink, eat, move, sleep, and so on. Reflect on time passing, and your own mortality. Try to get some perspective on yourself: a speck of protoplasm sitting in the grass, on a blue-and-white ball circling a minor star, swirling in its place in an immense galaxy that is itself just one of millions of galaxies. And yet your mind can encompass—get around and outside of—all those galaxies. In a very real way, you *are* the center of your universe.

Think of all the people you have known in your life. Each one human, each part of the dance of life, each just as insignificant, each just as able to encompass infinity in a thought, each the center of a universe.

Moral Inventory

A moral inventory is an honest, searching, fearless, and comprehensive description of yourself, including both the good and the bad. It involves searching your memory for your faults, failures, sins, crimes, vices, and weaknesses on the one hand, balanced by your virtues, successes, good deeds, positive traits, or strengths on the other hand.

Taking a personal moral inventory is the cornerstone of spiritual work for addicted people. It will build your powers of introspection, make you more honest, help you take responsibility for your actions, raise your self-confidence, and provide you with priceless self-knowledge. If you do only one exercise in this chapter, do this one.

There are six guidelines to follow:

Be honest. You want to see yourself as much as possible as you really are—not as you would like to believe you are, and not any worse than you really are. See yourself as a camera would see you, if there were a camera that could picture thoughts and actions as well as what you look like on the outside.

Be thorough. Take enough time to do as complete a job as you can.

Be realistic. Don't expect to do this perfectly. It's enough to make an honest beginning and simply to do your best.

Be responsible. Stick to your own attributes. Don't blame or analyze other people. Even in situations where you were the victim, focus on your own actions and feelings.

Be spontaneous. Put down the first things that come to mind. Don't erase or cross out anything. Don't edit your inventory.

Be positive. Put as much energy into exploring and listing your assets as you do your liabilities.

The following page contains an inventory form. Make enough photocopies to be able to have a separate form for everyone in your family, plus all your significant friends and acquaintances. The blank form is followed by an example of how one man filled out the form, focusing on his relationship with his wife. Save your inventory forms for later use in the chapters on communication and making amends.

Moral Inventory of Myself

In my relationship with _____

My Negative Attributes

What I did or didn't do: _____

_____

_____

_____ Fault or feeling: _____

What I did or didn't do: _____

_____

_____

_____ Fault or feeling: _____

What I did or didn't do: _____

_____

_____

_____ Fault or feeling: _____

What I did or didn't do: _____

_____

_____

_____ Fault or feeling: _____

What I did or didn't do: _____

_____

_____

_____ Fault or feeling: _____

My Positive Attributes

What I did or didn't do: _____

_____

_____

_____ Virtue or feeling: _____

What I did or didn't do: _____

_____

_____

_____ Virtue or feeling: _____

What I did or didn't do: _____

_____

_____

_____ Virtue or feeling: _____

What I did or didn't do: _____

_____

_____

_____ Virtue or feeling: _____

What I did or didn't do: _____

_____

_____

_____ Virtue or feeling: _____

Here are some suggestions that have helped others in making a good moral inventory:

In my relationship with. This can be your parents, siblings, spouse, children, friends, acquaintances, boss, co-workers. It can also be an organization, like a church, or a business or the government. You can complete the inventory for your relationship with people in general, such as the driving public whom you endangered when you drove drunk. Your inventory can even assess your behavior in relationship to a concept, such as truth or art or God or fidelity.

What I did or didn't do. Think about secrets, things you have never told anybody before. Look inside yourself for shame and guilt surrounding past actions or omissions that you regret. Think about situations that grew out of your drinking or drugging, but also think about your life experiences and tendencies before you ever started drinking or using drugs. Think about your relationships outside of the context of your drinking or drug use.

On the positive side, look for things you are proud of, areas of your life that have worked despite your addiction and other problems. In what ways have you been kind, generous, a good friend, a good listener? Spend as much time looking for your assets as you do cataloging your liabilities.

Fault/Virtue or feeling. Sum up your action or omission with one or two words that best describe the fault or the virtue exemplified. Or choose words that best describe how you felt in the situation. For example, If you borrowed money and didn't pay it back, you might write "irresponsibility," or "deceitfulness" if you never intended to repay the loan. Or you might call it "greed" or "using others." Your feelings might be described as "guilty" or "ashamed" or "a sense of failure." The words you choose should match your unique experience, even if they might not make complete sense to somebody else.

Summing up many different interactions with many different people will help you see patterns in your life. For example, you may begin to see that all your relationships have been influenced by your particular problems with insecurity or sexual desire or authority figures. Directing a separate inventory toward each of your relationships lends you the perspective of the other person involved. Viewing your life from these differing points of view—in other words, getting out of your own narcissistic bubble—is what introspection and self-knowledge are all about.

Here's an example of how Paul filled out one sheet of his inventory vis-à-vis his ex-wife Patty:

Moral Inventory of Myself

In my relationship with *Patty*

My Negative Attributes

What I did or didn't do: *Insisted on carrying her over the threshold on our wedding night, even though we were both too drunk. Broke her wrist.*

Fault or feeling: *Arrogance, Abuse*

What I did or didn't do: *Necking with our neighbor in my car outside our apartment, while Patty was inside partying.*

Fault or feeling: *Lust*

What I did or didn't do: *I'd get mad at the clutter of our lives and start throwing Patty's stuff away, especially magazines.*

Fault or feeling: *Anger*

What I did or didn't do: *Can't remember what Patty told me about the miscarriage she had before we were married, or the circumstances surrounding the time she got sick and went home to Utah to live.*

Fault or feeling: *Blackout, denial*

What I did or didn't do: *Drunk, on my way to get more beer for a party at our house, backed the car right over her dog and killed it.*

Fault or feeling: *Guilt*

My Positive Attributes

What I did or didn't do: *Supported us both while Patty went back to school.*

Virtue or feeling: *Generosity*

What I did or didn't do: *Wrote her love poems, brought flowers, courted her in a way she desperately needed and wanted, though it was foreign to me.*

Virtue or feeling: *Loving kindness, Empathy*

What I did or didn't do: *Despite many temptations and close calls, never actually slept with anyone else while we were married.*

Virtue or feeling: *Faithfulness*

What I did or didn't do: *Kept coming back, trying to make the marriage work, gradually focusing in on the role alcohol played in our relationship.*

Virtue or feeling: *Tenacity*

After completing one of these inventories for each of your significant relationships, you may feel exhausted, wrung out, shaky, guilty, exhilarated, energized, anxious, angry, or relieved. Strong feelings are to be expected from such searching self-analysis.

When you complete an inventory form, put it away for a couple of days. Then look at it again and make any additions or changes that occur to you. Save your inventories for use later, in the chapters on communication and making amends. But don't be in a rush to share this sensitive information with others. Wait until you are ready.

Building a Spiritual Family

Where can you find caring, helpful people to walk with you on this spiritual journey called recovery? Family and friends? Maybe. In a perfect world, we would all be reared in healthy families where there was nurturing and trust, where we could express all our feelings in safety, where communication was open and honest, and where our worth was affirmed. In such a family we would have felt free to become what we were meant to be.

Most of us were not that fortunate. Perhaps you find yourself facing up to your addiction without the support of either your family of origin or the family with which you now live. There is a high probability that your present circle of friends is not on the sidelines cheering your recovery effort. What you are doing may be very threatening to their own way of life, if they're into alcohol and drugs.

If you can't count on your real family and friends for the support you need, try constructing a spiritual family to call upon. The beauty of a spiritual family is that you are not limited to people you know. Spiritual family and friends don't have to be alive or even real.

Divide a piece of paper into two columns. In the first column, list all those traits you most admire, and would like to cultivate in yourself. Then, across from each trait, write the name of someone—living or dead, real or fictional—who personifies that trait for you. Label this second column, "Spiritual Family Member." Here's an example of how Tracy filled out her form:

Desired Trait	Spiritual Family Member
Acceptance	Helen Keller
Peace of Mind	Francis of Assisi
Patience	My grandmother
Courage	Martin Luther King
Energy	Bob Hope
Intelligence	Stephen Hawking
Humor	Garrison Keilor
Problem-Solving Skill	Lee Iaccoca
Faith	Mother Theresa

Daily Spiritual Practice

All religions and spiritual traditions recommend a daily spiritual practice, whether meditation, prayer, or ritual actions.

Anything that requires you to spend time quietly and alone, and to reflect each day can be a spiritual practice. For some the purpose is served by transcendental meditation, visualization, self-hypnosis, or yoga. For others it is served by writing in a diary or journal, taking a walk, listening to music, or tending a special garden or shrine.

In the early weeks and months of your recovery, reading and working in this book can serve as your spiritual practice. As you proceed to get free of drugs and alcohol, and heal your spiritual wounds, you can try different things in your search for a regular spiritual practice that suits you.

10

Communication

Recovery is all about becoming a successful adult with a rich, full, contented life, free of mood-altering chemicals. Successful adult living requires communication skills.

When you quit alcohol and drugs, you create some special communication problems for yourself. First, how do you tell your spouse, your family, and your friends that you're not drinking or using anymore?

Second, how do you talk to people in general as a newly sober, straight citizen, without the tongue-loosening inspiration of booze or pot or uppers? How do you converse when you're jumpy and irritable because of withdrawal symptoms, or later when you're shakily trying to put together a life without mind-bending chemicals?

Third, the spiritual work of recovering from addiction, especially conducting your moral inventory as you did in the last chapter, demands completion in the form of sharing your new insights about yourself with a trustworthy listener.

This chapter addresses all three of these special communication needs: talking about your sobriety, dealing spontaneously with others, and sharing your moral inventory.

Talking About Your Decision To Quit

Imagine walking into a big family get-together at Thanksgiving or somebody's birthday. Everybody's been there a while, liquor is flowing and the party is getting loud and happy. Your dad spots you, pulls you into the center of the circle, hands you an alcoholic drink, and says, "Here's to you—bottoms up."

What do you say? Write your response here:

_____

Imagine you're at a great party in your best friend's apartment. The music is good and loud, all your favorite people are here. Your friend draws you into the bedroom where the

inner circle, the coolest members of the in group, are gathered around a misty mirror, snorting lines of pharmacologically pure cocaine. Your best friend hands you a straw.
What do you say? Write your response here:

_____

Imagine you're working in the hot sun. You are tired, sore, hot, and thirsty. You set your tools down and trudge toward the house. As you walk up the steps into the shade of the porch, somebody cracks open a can of beer and hands it to you. It's ice cold in your hand, the condensation running down the metal sides, the frosty smell of your favorite brew wafting upwards. What do you say? Write your response here:

_____

Imagine you are at your favorite restaurant with your lover, eating your favorite dish. Your lover sips fine vintage wine and says, "This is the best Cabernet I've ever had. You just have to try a sip. It's a once-in-a-lifetime opportunity."
What do you say? Write your response here:

_____

If you had a hard time coming up with responses to these imaginary situations, you should plan right now what you will say when you encounter similar situations in real life. Here are some suggestions to get you started. Practice saying your responses out loud, until they become easy, natural, and automatic.

I quit.

I don't drink.

I don't drink anymore.

I stopped for health reasons.

My liver can't take it.

I get nose bleeds.

I'm allergic to it.

It was taking over too much of my life.

It was making me crazy, I had to stop.

I had to stop drinking to stay out of jail.

I nearly killed myself with that stuff.

I stopped to save my job.

I quit to save my relationship.

I promised myself I wouldn't.

I was afraid I'd hurt somebody.

My doctor told me to stop.

It saps my energy.

It makes me too uptight.

I'm trying to set a good example for my kids.

It kills my creativity.

I need to keep my mind sharp.

I quit to get back in control of my life

I'm taking medications—I can't touch a drop.

I'm the designated driver.

Things are bad enough—that would only make them worse.

I have a lot to do tomorrow.

I'd rather dance.

I have to get up early in the morning.

I'm on the wagon.

I've already had my share.

Add your own responses you'd like to use.

_____

_____

_____

_____

_____

_____

When people are persistent, you can say:

If it bothers you so much that I'm not drinking, maybe I'd better be going. See you later.

Look, it's not something I want to argue about. This is a very important decision I've made, and I expect you, as someone who cares about me, to respect it.

I don't expect you to support me in this, or even to understand—but it's a decision I'm bound and determined to stick by. So if you keep bugging me, I'm not going to spend time with you anymore.

Are there other responses that you think would work well with your family and friends? Add them here.

_____

_____

_____

_____

_____

For example, Lynn had gone two months without a drink or a sleeping pill when she received the invitation to her sister's wedding. She knew there would be lots of champagne and beer and brandy at the reception. She knew she would feel like a failure because she was a single, unemployed college drop-out, while her younger sister had always been an A student, made good money in real estate, and was marrying a nice guy from a wealthy, respected family.

Lynn knew that the urge to drink would be strong. Her brothers and cousins would expect her to get bombed with them, maybe sneak outside to smoke a joint or two, then sit on the sidelines cracking sarcastic jokes about the guests. She felt that she had to attend the wedding and the reception, but she was determined to resist all invitations to drink.

Lynn practiced in front of a mirror, looking directly into her own eyes, saying:

I quit drinking last March

I don't drink anymore.

I'd really rather have punch.

For insistent cousins and brothers who kidded her and egged her on, she prepared these statements:

Help me out—I really can't drink anymore.

Alcohol's poison to me now. Stop pushing it on me.

If all else failed, she planned to escape into the ladies room, or got talk to her teetotaler Uncle Clarence about his greenhouse. She managed to survive the reception, armed with her rehearsed phrases. She even got to play an unaccustomed role near the end of the reception, when her slightly tipsy sister caught her spike heel in the hem of her bridal veil and almost fell. Lynn steadied her sister helping her into the limo, then whispered to their mother, "She'll be all right—she just had a little too much to drink."

Any excuse that preserves your sobriety is okay. Just make sure you don't start believing your own white lies. For example, you might tell your nosy aunt Maisie, "I've decided to lighten up for a while" when she offers you a highball. That's okay, because you only see her once a year. But beware of telling everybody around you things like:

I'm on the wagon tonight.

I'm cutting back.

I'm drying out this week.

By implying that your decision to quit alcohol or drugs is casual or temporary, you may be giving yourself an out—an excuse so that you can start drinking or drugging again later, claiming that "I never said I was quitting for good."

If you've quit for good—if you know in your heart that you don't have any business drinking or drugging ever again—say so. Especially say so to the people who count most in your life. There is nothing wrong with the statement, "I don't drink."

Dealing With Others Spontaneously

It can be very painful talking to "normal" people when you're going through detox. Every nerve ending is raw. Everything is so annoying, so difficult, so confusing. Even later, when you are past the withdrawal symptoms, social gatherings can be pure torture without a drink or a drag to get you in the mood.

You need a simple formula to get started talking to people, something to fall back on that's easy to remember and easy to use. Just follow this outline, regardless of the topic of conversation, and you will come across as a close approximation of a human being, and perhaps even enjoy yourself:

I think _____

I feel _____

I want _____

This formula contains the essential ingredients of human discourse: opinion, emotion, and desire.

The *I think* part should be your opinion, observation, or analysis. If you have no opinion about something, just make one up or admit that you are ambivalent. You're after verbal quantity here, not sincerity or brilliance.

The *I feel* part should be your emotional response to the topic—how you feel about it. If you get stuck here, remember that the primary emotions are joy, fear, anger, and sadness. Just pick one at random and apply it to the topic at hand.

The *I want* part is an expression of your preference or desire. It usually follows logically from your thoughts and feelings. It's what makes you an individual. Expressing your wants is a crucial factor in getting others to understand you and meet some of your needs.

Here are some examples of how this formula works in all sorts of conversations:

Movies

I think his movies are too violent.

I feel queasy and sick with all that blood spraying around.

I want to see characters I care about, with realistic problems they can solve without whipping out a sawed-off shotgun.

Kids

I think Tracy's too young to stay out all night.

I feel scared for her safety.

I want her to get in by 2 A.M.

Breaking up

I think we have a mutually destructive relationship.

I feel sad and scared when I think about breaking up, but

I want to move out.

Drinking

I feel out of control when I'm drinking.

I think I'm an alcoholic.

I want to stop for good, but

I'm afraid I don't have the willpower.

I think I'm going to need a lot of help.

I want your support, because

I know I can trust you.

This last example shows that you don't have to follow a rigid *think/feel/want* sequence. You don't have to use the exact words "think," "feel," and "want"; you can string several sequences together to express complex thoughts, feelings, and requests quite eloquently.

These examples are pared down and simplified. In actual conversation, there are more interruptions, questions, and changes of subject. Don't worry if you compose a perfect *I think/I feel/I want* sequence and you get interrupted and never get to complete it. The main thing is to memorize the formula, and use it at those times when you feel tongue-tied and isolated in a social setting, or in an intimate conversation.

Try your hand at the formula. Pick a topic that your friends typically discuss, preferably one that you find boring or pointless. Write down two *I think/I feel/I want* statements that you can contribute the next time the subject comes up:

I think _____

I feel _____

I want _____

I think _____

I feel _____

I want _____

Sharing Your Moral Inventory

The fifth step of the twelve steps of Alcoholics Anonymous talks about admitting "to God, to ourselves, and to another human being the exact nature of our wrongs." AA members speak of "clearing away the wreckage of the past." This section is organized along similar lines. It involves sharing your insights about your liabilities and assets with another human being.

Part of the spiritual dilemma of addiction is how it keeps you from knowing yourself, and thus from letting others know you. In the last chapter you began a moral inventory of all your significant relationships. You cataloged your wrong doings and your virtues so that you could get a clearer, more honest picture of yourself.

The next task in your spiritual undertaking is to share that picture with someone else. Find someone you trust to just listen to you and keep what you say to him- or herself. This can be a friend, a minister, a counselor, an AA sponsor, someone you have known for a long time, or a recent acquaintance you have come to respect and trust. Your spouse, or others with whom you have powerful emotional bonds, are probably not a wise choice of partner in this task.

When you think you have picked the right person, ask him or her in a clear, direct way:

As part of my addiction recovery I've made a moral inventory of my life, the good and the bad. I need to talk to somebody about it. Would you be willing to listen to my story?

If the response is initially positive, go on to arrange a good time and a quiet place where there will be no interruptions:

I could come over tomorrow night if you're not busy. Or we could go to the cafe and get a quiet table.

Start by asking the person to keep everything you say in confidence, and to listen without comment, unless they need to ask questions for clarity:

Before I get started, I should tell you that this is very confidential. Some of this stuff I've never told anybody—embarrassing and illegal stuff. I want to make sure you're willing to keep it all secret.

I'll try to just tell you my story from beginning to end. If something's not clear and you don't understand, you should ask questions. But mostly I'd like you to just listen and save any comments till the end.

Of course, you'll want to adjust the language of these statements to fit your individual style.

When planning how to tell your story, it helps to follow one main organizing principle. You can organize your story by time, by person, or by character traits.

If you choose a chronological organization, start early in time with your childhood and relationships with your family of origin, and proceed from there to your teen years, leaving home, and so on.

If you choose to organize your material by person, start with your most important relationship, and tell everything about you and that person. Then proceed to the next most important person, and so on.

If you choose to organize things by character trait, pick your most characteristic trait, and give examples from various times and relationships in your life. For example:

Fear has dominated my life. I was afraid of my abusive dad and uncle, so I tried to be invisible and perfect. In grammar school I was afraid of the nuns, so I became the perfect little student for them. In college I was afraid of being fat, so I made myself sick with every new diet that came along. I was afraid of being alone and unpopular, so I became the perfect party girl. My first boyfriend Freddy raped me on our first date, but I was so afraid of rejection I pretended it was all right—just a little too much beer and hormones. The more afraid I got, the more I drank and screwed around, and the more I drank and screwed around, the more afraid I got.

Sometimes I cover the fear with anger and rebellion. I ran away from home eventually. I took up noble causes like peace and the rain forest. When I was righteously angry about some injustice or stupidity, I didn't feel the fear so much.

Notice that this story is organized by feelings—fear and then anger. But the examples of each feeling are organized by time, from earliest to latest occurrences. This helps your listener follow the story and helps you remember everything.

It's a very good idea to make notes and take them with you. The stress of revealing long-withheld secrets can make your memory very unreliable. You don't have to write out your moral inventory word-for-word and read it; but an outline of key people, events, and times will help enormously.

Stress what *you* did or failed to do, not what other people did to you or failed to do for you. Don't go into what you wish you had done or what you plan to do to make amends. Stick to the facts of your own behavior. Try not to apologize or explain or justify.

In the course of sharing your moral inventory, you're going to feel embarrassed, vulnerable, exposed, scared, sad, angry—a whole range of feelings are possible. When feelings come up, acknowledge them to your listener:

> *I'm feeling really sad as I tell you about my first wife. I made so many mistakes, and it's too late to fix them. It just makes me want to cry.*

Include your assets. You want to present a balanced picture of yourself, not heap ashes on your head in an orgy of self-vilification. It's not bragging to list your good points and give some examples:

> *All the time I was doing cocaine and speed, even when my life was falling apart, I stayed true to my artistic commitments. I kept painting and sculpting. A lot of it was hopeless raving, but I kept doing it, even when my hand was shaking so bad I couldn't hold the brush or the knife steady. Somehow I always finished my commissions, and never missed an opening.*

Tell your listener when you're finished, and invite feedback. Be attentive and open to what the other person has to say, and thank him or her for hearing you out.

After sharing yourself like this, you'll probably feel very close and grateful to your listener. You may also feel raw and exposed, or warm and comforted. You may feel that it didn't go well, or that it was better than you ever dreamed it could be. You may find yourself entertaining several contradictory feelings at the same time.

Tell yourself ahead of time that whatever you feel at the end, you will accept it as natural and normal for you. You won't let it invalidate the experience for you. You won't judge or blame yourself.

Whatever you feel, remember to congratulate yourself for having the courage and tenacity to take a major step on your path to recovery.

11

Making Amends

This chapter will guide you in planning and making amends to the people in your life you have injured, insulted, cheated, abandoned, neglected, or otherwise wronged. Making amends is important in recovery, not only because it is right and just, but also because it is critical that you make an attempt to repair the damage of the past.

You can make amends for things you *did* like hitting your kids, wrecking the car, or stealing money. Or you can make amends for things you *failed to do,* like missing your son's graduation, not making child-support payments, or reneging on contracts or promises.

Making amends does not mean apologizing. Making amends means *doing something* to make up, at least in part, for past wrongs. You can

- Give money

- Return goods

- Keep broken promises

- Volunteer your labor

- Tell the truth to someone you lied to

- Admit you were in the wrong

- Give time and emotional support to someone you neglected

- Break off a harmful relationship and stay completely out of that person's life

Emotional, Spiritual, and Social Benefits

Making amends is the logical continuation of work you have begun in previous chapters. In the chapter on spirituality, you conducted a moral inventory, admitting your strengths and weaknesses to yourself. In the communication chapter, you shared your inventory with someone else, validating new insights, and gaining experience in communicating important facts about yourself.

The next step is to admit your failings to the people whom you've hurt, and to offer reparations. This is difficult work. It can be very embarrassing and painful. It stirs up memories that you might greatly prefer to leave dormant.

But making amends is worth it. You can reap enormous emotional, spiritual, and social benefits. On the emotional side, you can relieve a lot of the guilt and shame surrounding some of your most painful memories.

The spiritual benefit of making amends is the rehabilitation of your moral health. When you stopped putting mood-altering chemicals into your body, you began to rehabilitate your physical health, improving your stamina, digestion, mental clarity, the quality of your sleep, and so on. Righting the wrongs you have done is the beginning of a moral rehabilitation program, in which you will strengthen your values of honesty, humility, justice, and responsibility.

The social benefits of making amends include becoming less isolated from your family and friends. You can begin to repair the social contract between yourself and the rest of humanity that your drinking or drug use has strained. Not only will you become somewhat closer to people you already know, but you will also form new relationships more easily as you begin to interact more honestly and responsibly with people.

Photocopy the form on the following page. Make one copy for each person to whom you need to make amends.

Write each person's name at the top of a blank form. If you already did the moral inventory in the spirituality chapter, you will have already identified all the people you have harmed.

If the total of all the people you've harmed seems like too many to deal with at once, limit your list to those who are most important and accessible to you—those you hurt the most, who are still alive, whom you still see, who haven't moved far away, and so on.

Here's a helpful hint: If you find yourself fantasizing about making amends to somebody you knew long ago, but you tell yourself, "No, it's all in the past," you probably need to make amends to that person. Even if you can't track the person down, you can at least make symbolic amends by writing an unmailed letter.

Don't forget yourself—you can make amends for what you've done to harm yourself. You've already begun this process by quitting alcohol or drugs.

Make a List of What You Did or Failed To Do

Write down what you did or failed to do that caused harm to each person for whom you've made a form. Obvious examples are physical or material harm, such as

- Stealing money

- Cheating

- Failing to honor legal or contractual obligations

- Hitting or bullying people

Amends

To be made to: _____

What I did or failed to do: _____
_____
_____
_____

How I can forgive myself: _____
_____
_____
_____

Old grudges or rationalizations I need to let go of: _____
_____
_____

What I could do to make amends: _____
_____
_____

Statement of amends: _____
_____
_____
_____
_____
_____
_____

- Damaging property

- Being sexually abusive

- Failing to provide financial support

Don't forget mental, moral, emotional, or spiritual kinds of harm. These involve such actions as

- Lying

- Making false promises

- Breaking faith

- Setting a bad example for young people

- Sexual infidelity

- Verbal abuse

- Unfair criticism or nagging

- Actions spurred by jealousy or envy

- Sexual harassment

- Inattention to loved ones

- Making false accusations

- Emotional coldness

- Skimping on obligations

- Lack of gratitude

- Arrogance

- Not encouraging those who need encouragement

- Behaving in a way that's humiliating to yourself or others

Forgive Yourself

It's a spiritual truism that to be forgiven you have to forgive yourself. If you can forgive yourself for what you did or failed to do, check this item off and move on. If self-forgiveness is difficult for you, spend some time trying to find a way to forgive yourself.

Remember that true forgiveness is not forgetting or total absolution. It isn't a matter of dismissing grievous wrongs, or making them okay. Rather it's a matter of admitting that you are a flawed human being, that at the time you were impaired by chemical substances, under stress, or out of control.

True evil is extremely rare. If you were truly evil, you would not be reading this book. You would not care about making amends. The bad things you have done in the past were most likely predictable mistakes, given your low level of awareness at the time. However misguided your actions, and horrible the consequences, you were trying to do the best you could to survive.

Psychologists who study human motivation point out that we automatically seek pleasure and avoid pain. It's a built-in survival mechanism. All individuals, at any given moment, are doing what seems most likely to them to ensure their survival. When you are physically, mentally, and morally damaged by drugs or alcohol, your perceptions of the circumstances can be so warped that you make some wretched and disastrous choices. You decide that driving your car is better than calling a cab. You decide that you can beat up a barroom full of loggers. You decide that you should give in to your sexual attraction to your child's babysitter. You decide to teach your spouse a lesson once and for all.

You can take responsibility for what you did, but still forgive yourself—because you were doing your miserable best. You need to forgive yourself so that you can move forward on your spiritual path. Shame and guilt over the past are fruitless and paralyzing. A more appropriate feeling is one of responsibility for what you do from now on.

Let Go of Grudges

It's likely that some of the people you have harmed have also harmed you. Especially in alcoholic families, there is plenty of abuse, neglect, abandonment, and betrayal to go around. Parents, children, and siblings all take their turns as victims and transgressors over the years.

Leftover hurt and anger will not only get in the way of making amends, they can also endanger your recovery. Resentment over past hurts is a major cause of relapse. So to protect your recovery, and properly make amends, you are going to have to let go of some of the grudges you hold.

Keep telling yourself that the goal of making amends is one-sided. It's about *you* owning up to *your* wrongdoings, and offering compensation for them. You can't be concerned with the other person's wrongdoings, or the other person's reaction to you. Let go of blame and any idea of finally setting the record straight about who did what to whom.

Likewise, you might have a list of rationalizations that you habitually trot out whenever the subject of your failings comes up. You missed your daughter's wedding because the plane was overbooked, and they told you the wrong gate number—it had nothing to do with the five highballs you had in the airport bar. You really can't be blamed for drinking away your job—the boss always had it in for you, and would have fired you no matter what you did. You never would have got a DUI if you hadn't been driving your brother-in-law's foreign car with the confusing gear shift. And so on.

Now is the time to carefully examine your old rationalizations and let them go. Admit that you screwed up. Take full responsibility for the facts of your mistakes, and let the extenuating circumstances fade into the drunken fog that spawned them.

What You Can Do To Make Amends

For each person you've harmed, determine what you might do to make amends. There are several ways to make amends. You can make direct, complete amends by paying old debts, or returning stolen money or property. You can pay to replace damaged property. You can add on extra money or goods to compensate for mental anguish or lost interest—what a court of law would call punitive damages. You might make partial amends if you just don't have enough money to make full restitution. You might set up an installment plan to pay off old debts.

The best amends are both direct and logically related to the original insult or injury. Here are some examples:

- Stealing money—pay it back

- Cheating—return ill-gotten gains

- Failing to honor legal or contractual obligations—honor them or pay compensation

- Hitting or shoving people—reimburse medical bills

- Damaging property—fix it

- Being sexually abusive—pay for therapy

- Failing to provide financial support—provide it now

- Lying—tell the truth

- Making false promises—do what you said you'd do

- Breaking faith—honor your commitment

- Setting a bad example for young people—set a good example

- Sexual infidelity—own up to what you did; resolve to be faithful in the future

- Verbal abuse—acknowledge it as such; be an ego builder, not an ego destroyer

- Unfair criticism or nagging—look for the positive, give praise

- Actions spurred by jealousy or envy—express trust, compliments on good fortune

- Sexual harassment—admit to your actions; resolve to treat others with dignity and respect

- Inattention to loved ones—start paying attention

- Making false accusations—acknowledge the truth

- Emotional coldness—give hugs and compliments

- Skimping on obligations—attend to all your obligations

- Lack of gratitude—give sincere thank yous

- Arrogance—practice careful listening and appreciation

- Embarrassing self and others—act appropriately, with dignity

- Not encouraging those who need encouragement—be generous in your encouragement and praise

Unfortunately, it's often too late to make simple, direct amends. If you've been neglecting and abusing your family and friends and co-workers for years and years, you will have to make indirect or partial amends. For example, there may be no way to restore a lost life or damaged reputation, but you can give money or aid to an injured person's family, friends, or favorite charity. You can donate your labor to someone's pet project.

You can make amends overtly, with everyone knowing what the compensation is for. Or in some cases, you might have to make covert, secret amends, to avoid doing further harm. Part of the process of making amends is to figure out how to act without doing further harm.

For example, years ago Ruth slept with her best friend Rita's husband, Ralph. Rita never found out about it, and she and Ralph are still more or less happily married. There is no way of making direct amends now without causing more harm. Telling the truth now would hurt both Rita and Ralph more than the three of them would be benefited by a more honest basis to their relationship. The best Ruth could do was to have a quiet talk with Ralph, explaining that she had been wrong to sleep with him, and had absolutely no intention of repeating the mistake. The best amends Ruth could make to Rita were indirect and partial: doing her favors, watching her kids, supporting her in crises, looking out for her best interests, and so on—being the best friend she could be, and living with her secret. Making amends is sometimes a delicate task of moral judgment.

Sometimes you won't be able to make amends in person. Or a situation is so complicated, and feelings run so high, that personal confrontation will seem too potentially volatile. In such cases, it can be best to write a letter. In a letter you can take your time, organize your thoughts, and present your feelings in a way that won't overwhelm either you or the recipient. A letter can be read over and over again, before and after you mail it. This is why a telephone call is such an inadequate alternative—you may speak in haste, and the person you're calling can hang up on you. When you send the best letter you're able to write, there's a good chance that your message will come across—if not on the first reading, then perhaps on the third or fourth.

In other cases, the key players may be dead, senile, moved with no forwarding address, or otherwise unreachable. Even if this is so, a letter is still a good idea. You will get 90 percent of the value of making amends, even though you can't mail your letter. Writing an unmailed letter is also a good plan when you can't make direct amends to someone in a vulnerable position, but you still want to get all the facts and feelings clear in your mind.

Statement of Amends

For each person, write out a statement of amends in advance. Try to fit it into this format:

I was _____

         (drunk, high, hung over)

when _____

happened between us.

I regret the pain I caused you.

I ask your forgiveness for anything else I did to hurt you.

I want to make amends by _____ .

                              (what you plan to do)

For example, here is Joyce's statement of amends to her younger sister:

I was drunk when we were going through Mama's stuff after she died. I lied to you about not being able to find her photo album and her wedding ring—I kept them for myself. I regret lying to you, and stealing from you. I ask your forgiveness for that and for anything else I did to cause you pain. I want to make amends by giving the ring and the pictures to you now.

Keep your statements simple, with no blame and no excuses. Making amends does not mean apologizing or justifying. You might include an apology in a statement of amends, but the focus should be on what you plan to do to make up for the wrongs you have done.

When, Where, and How To Make Amends

Choose when, where, and how to make amends to each person. To do this, sort all your amends forms into four piles:

Pile 1. Those who are accessible to you now, to whom you can make amends right away, in person.

Pile 2. People who are less accessible or inaccessible because they are gone, lost, dead, and so on. To these people you will write a letter and either mail it or not.

Pile 3. People who would be harmed by complete disclosure. You can write unmailed letters to these people, and figure out how to make indirect amends later.

Pile 4. People at whom you're still too angry to want to make amends, or who are still too angry at you to accept your amends in any form. Try to rid yourself of these old grudges and rationalizations. Postpone making amends to the people in this pile, but not forever. Don't use this category as an excuse for procrastination. Pile 4 should be very small, containing forms for no more than one or two people.

Pick the least difficult person from Pile 1 and make amends. If you aren't ready to jump right into a confrontation, practice what you will say by visualizing the scene in your imagination. You can also speak your piece in front of a mirror; or get a trusted friend or AA sponsor to play the part of the person you hurt, so that you can practice what you want to say.

After the least difficult person is dealt with, move on to someone a little more difficult. Work your way through the piles in order. This will take a long time. It may be the hardest but most rewarding work you have ever done.

Take What You Get

Accept whatever response you get to your attempts to make amends. Be prepared for anything: hugs, tears, outrage, indifference, forgiveness, reconciliation, jokes, sneers, or embarrassment.

Before you approach someone to make amends, tell yourself:

I'm willing to love and forgive both myself and the other person involved. I take responsibility for what I'm going to say. I intend to humbly make amends in the best way I can. I'm willing to live with the outcome, whatever happens. The process of making amends is what counts, not any particular response from the other person.

Some relationships are so toxic, so ruined, so steeped in failure that no amount of amends on your part can fix them. In such cases, you will have to be content with the spiritual benefits accruing to the process of offering amends. You are in control over what you do and say, but you have no control over how the other person will respond.

Example

Here is how Marilyn worked out her amends to her estranged friend and business partner Betty:

Amends

To be made to:
Betty

What I did or failed to do:
Stole money, drank in the store, closed early, falsified the books.

How I can forgive myself:
I was out of control, in a fog, doing the best I could to survive my addiction.

Old grudges or rationalizations I need to let go of:
Told myself Betty was cheap, that it was just a loan, that I would pay it all back before she noticed. But it was theft, plain and simple.

What I could do to make amends:
Return some money and antiques. Offer to help out free of charge in Betty's new store to help pay back the rest of what I owe her.

Amends statement

I was drinking a lot when we opened the antique store on Main Street. I kept a bottle of brandy stashed in that pine commode we could never sell, and I was drunk in the store most afternoons. It's my fault that business failed. I was pocketing money when I was there alone and customers paid in cash. I fiddled the account books hoping you'd never notice. Some days I just closed early and staggered home.

I regret wrecking our business, and I regret even more hurting our friendship. When you opened your new store without me, I knew you must suspect something. You were right not to trust me.

I ask your forgiveness for all that, and for anything else I did to cause you pain.

I want to make amends by giving you this check for $600, and donating my cherry lap desk to your inventory. Also, if you ever need help in your new store, I'd be glad to do cleaning or refinishing or anything, no charge. I've been off alcohol for nine months now, and I'm determined never to drink again.

Marilyn practiced her speech in front of a mirror. She imagined Betty having all sorts of reactions, and saw herself in her mind's eye continuing to speak calmly and clearly, right to the end. Marilyn's AA sponsor went over the wording with her, and made several suggestions.

Marilyn called Betty, and asked if they could meet at the store after closing. Marilyn showed up with the check in hand, and the cherry lap desk in her car. She cried when she spoke her piece, and they were both in tears by the end. Betty said that she was glad it was all out in the open at last, and forgave Marilyn.

Six months later, Marilyn was watching the store for Betty every Wednesday afternoon. One Wednesday she sold her own cherry lap desk to a man from Spokane for $300. Since Betty had never cashed her $600 check, Marilyn quietly slipped $900 into the till.

Special Considerations

Never attempt to make amends when there is a chance of harming others. Confessing old infidelities may make you feel better, yet cause great pain to those who were betrayed.

Nor is there much point in owning up to past criminal behavior. Repaying victims is a must, yes. But going to prison won't help you or your family. Unless someone else has been falsely accused of what you did, it is best to put past crimes behind you, and make amends to society by a life well lived in the present and future.

12

Relapse Prevention

Many of the chapters in this book contribute to relapse prevention: improving your nutrition, exercise, dealing with feelings, spiritual work, improving communication, making amends, and so on. But this is the only chapter that focuses exclusively on what happens when you return to drinking or drugging, and how to prevent it.

Dozens of studies by addiction researchers have tracked alcoholics and drug addicts to see how many relapse, when they relapse, and how many relapsed addicts return to abstinence. From all these studies, three general conclusions can be drawn. First, you're most likely to relapse in the first three months after quitting. Second, your overall chance of relapsing is about 50-50. Third, a relapse is not the end of the world—it is part of the natural cycle of change, a step on the way to lasting recovery.

The natural cycle of change looks like this:

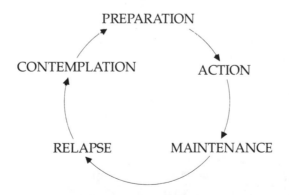

This pattern holds true for all changes: stopping a cocaine habit, deciding to get married, buying a new car, dyeing your hair. You start with contemplation—should you quit cocaine or not? Then you prepare by talking to a trusted friend, reading a magazine article, trying a day or two without drugs. You move into action and quit, getting rid of all drug paraphernalia, shunning certain people and places and parties. You suffer through withdrawal and enter the maintenance phase of actually living without cocaine. But after a while the novelty and pride of living drug-free fades, you enter a stressful period of your life, temptation comes your way, and you relapse and take a couple of lines at a party. Soon you're getting high every chance you get.

But even as you slide into your old ways, you watch yourself. You quickly enter the contemplation mode: how is it going? Is it getting as bad as the last time? As soon as you ask yourself, "Should I quit again?" you're back in the preparation stage, and the cycle continues. After two or three trips around the cycle, you enter a drug-free maintenance phase that lasts the rest of your life.

With luck—and the skills you can learn in this chapter—you can make your current maintenance phase the final one that lasts the rest of your life.

How Relapse Happens

On the surface, relapse seems simple: you're tempted, you want to drink or drug, so you give in and do it. But in reality, relapse is not so simple a matter. It involves a long string of steps, with opportunities to intervene at several points along the way.

Here's how relapse works:

Something happens. This can be an event, a situation, a person from the past, a mood. It can be anything, good or bad, inside you or outside you. You get a notice from the finance company that they're going to repossess your car. You win the lottery. You go to a party and the old gang are whooping it up, getting loaded while you sit on the sidelines with club soda and lime. You think about lost loves and lost chances. You see a movie that makes you cry. You feel especially alive and strong one day.

You interpret it. The thing that happens triggers a deep core belief about yourself and the world that you originally formed in childhood:

I'm a failure.
They're all against me.
I must have my way.
I'm worthless.
There's danger everywhere.
I'm incompetent.
I'm unlovable.
Life's unfair.
I'm a misfit.
People are no good.

The core belief helps you interpret the thing that happened in the form of automatic thoughts:

This will ruin me.
There's no hope.

It's awful.
I'm going crazy.
I'm going to die.
I can't stand it.
What's the use of trying?
I can do anything I want.

Interpretations give rise to cravings.

I'd like to have a drink . . . right now.
Let's do a line.
I need a joint.
Maybe I should take a pill or two.

Cravings inspire permission-giving thoughts.

It will calm me down.
One won't hurt.
What the hell—everything else is going wrong.
I'm strong now—I can handle it.
Just for medicinal purposes . . .
I deserve to celebrate.
I need to forget.
I've been sober a long time—it's out of my system.

You focus on action. This is when you head for the beer in the refrigerator, drive to the liquor store, rummage in your roommates' closets looking for their stash, drift to the rear bathroom where the cokeheads hang out, get in line at the cash bar at a reception, look for the waiter, and so on.

You drink or take the drug. At the end of this long string of events, you finally crack open the beer and drink it, toss back the shot of bourbon, sip the Margarita, light the joint, snort the line, pop the pill, or otherwise use the substance from which you've been abstaining.

Here is what the sequence looks like in a diagram:

Something Happens
|
Beliefs/Thoughts
|
Cravings
|
Permission-giving Thoughts
|
Focus on Action
|
Drink or Drug

In the depths of chemical dependency, this whole sequence is unconscious, almost completely out of your awareness. You open the repossession notice from the finance company, and magically find yourself with a beer in your hand. You walk into the old gang's party, and a scotch and soda materializes before you. You remember the pain of breaking up with your lover, and the doobie seems to roll itself. You hear certain music, see strobe lights on dancing bodies, and that white powder just jumps up your nose.

It's this introspective blindness that allows you to say, "Hey, there's no problem—I can quit any time," when it's obvious to others that you're out of control.

As you move toward sobriety, you become more aware of the internal sequence. You wake up and start noticing your cravings or the actions you typically take to get drugs or alcohol. You start observing the sequence. You experiment with interrupting it. This is the contemplation and preparation part of quitting. Finally you make the big change and quit.

A Five-Step Program for Relapse Prevention

Relapse prevention is a matter of continuing to do what you have already successfully begun. It's just more systematic. What you need to learn to do is improve your skill at stopping the relapse process at any of the five steps before the final "Drink or Drug" step. You can:

1. Stop something from happening

2. Redirect action

3. Contradict permission-giving thoughts

4. Cope with cravings

5. Change core beliefs and automatic thoughts

1. Stop Something From Happening

Although you can't control random events, you *can* identify your own high-risk situations and avoid them. For those you can't avoid, you can plan how you will handle them without relapsing. This is the most important step to master in the first few months of sobriety.

In the space provided below, list the situations that you know in advance will tempt you to take a drink or use drugs. Think of both negative and positive situations. Think of external events as well as internal feelings and memories.

High-Risk Situations

	External	**Internal**
Negative	_____	_____
	_____	_____
	_____	_____
	_____	_____
	_____	_____
Positive	_____	_____
	_____	_____
	_____	_____
	_____	_____

When you've listed all the high-risk situations you can think of, go through the list, and circle the ones you can avoid entirely. These are likely to be the "external positives," such as favorite bars, certain parties, old neighborhoods where you scored drugs, and certain people you can't afford to hang out with anymore. Resolve to avoid these people and places like the proverbial plague. They are deadly for you.

For the rest of the list, the unavoidable risks, you'll need to move on to the other steps in formulating your coping strategies.

Here's an example of how Harry filled out his list of high-risk situations:

High-Risk Situations

	External	**Internal**
Negative	Boss nags at me	Depressed
	Tax audit	Brooding over first marriage
	Crummy neighborhood	Tired after work
	Bills	Lonely
	(Visit from junky sister)	Bored, nervous
	Phone call from son	Arthritis acts up
Positive	Win $20 lottery ticket	Happy tax audit's over
	Get a promotion	Feeling flush on payday
	(Favorite sports bar)	
	Bob's retirement party	
	(Jane says come over)	

Harry circled his sister, his ex-girlfriend Jane, and Monday night football at the local sports bar—people and places that he should simply avoid. He told his sister that he wouldn't be available for visiting this summer. He told Jane that if she really wanted to get together just to talk, they could meet in the morning somewhere for coffee—he couldn't risk coming over to her apartment with its well-stocked bar, and their history of getting bombed during their "discussions." He invited a guy he met at an AA meeting to come over on Monday night to watch football and drink Cokes.

2. Redirect Action

This is really a two-step process. The first step is to clean up your environment so that drugs and alcohol aren't easily accessible to you. The second step is to prepare a list of alternate activities, so that when you feel cravings you can have something else to do besides drinking or taking drugs.

Cleaning up your environment. The best thing you can do is to get rid of all alcohol and drugs in your home. That means all of it, even the special bottle you thought you would save for guests, the souvenir miniatures from your Hawaii vacation, the grain alcohol swiped from the chemistry lab that you're saving for disinfectant, the stems and buds at the bottom of the drawer, the burnt-out roaches in the ashtrays, the leftover prescriptions for sleeping pills or tranquilizers, the cough syrup that gives you a buzz, and so on down the line. If it alters consciousness, get rid of it.

If people in your home still drink or do drugs, get them to at least keep it out of sight. Put the liquor bottles in a cupboard instead of leaving them out on the counter. Don't buy liquor for the rest of the family when you shop—make them buy their own. Train everybody around you to stop automatically offering you drinks. Take yourself out of the alcohol and drug loop as much as possible.

Alternate activities. List alternative activities that you can do to take up the time you used to spend drinking and drugging. Most important are things you can do any time you feel cravings. Here are some suggestions to get you started. Add your own ideas at the bottom of each list.

Things you can do almost any time

- Step outside for a breath of air

- Take a walk

- Write a little in your journal

- Stretching, deep breathing, relaxation exercises

- Clean house

- Reorganize a drawer or cupboard

- Work in your garden—pull weeds, plant something

- Read an inspirational passage

- Yoga exercises

- Call a friend

- Do some work in this or another self-help book

- Turn on the radio or TV

- Listen to music

- Say a prayer or affirmation

- Meditate

- Strike up a conversation

- Do someone a small favor

- Work on craft project

- Sing or play a musical instrument

- Read the newspaper

- Take a bath or shower

- Fix your makeup

- Have a snack

- Take your kid or a friend's kid to a playground or a kid's movie

- _____

- _____

- _____

Physical Activities

- Play tennis, basketball, soccer, or participate in other sports

- Take exercise, dance, Tai Chi, or yoga classes

- Put on a tape and dance in your living room

- Work out at a gym

- Work out on an exercise machine in your home

- Go hiking, jogging, swimming

- Go sailing, canoeing, kayaking

- Go bowling

- _____

- _____

- _____

Creative Activities, Hobbies

- Draw, paint, or sculpt

- Play or compose music

- Practice photography

- Write in a journal

- Write poetry, fiction, essays

- Do crafts

- Work on collections

- Put photographs in an album

- Sew

- Cook

- Build models

- Work and play on your computer

- Play video games

- Do woodworking

- Flying

- _____

- _____

- _____

Intellectual/Spiritual Activities

- Take classes, work toward a degree

- Read books

- Visit museums, attend lectures

- Work on your resume

- Teach

- Attend church services

- Meditate
- Pray and reflect
- _____
- _____
- _____

Social Activities

- Join AA
- Participate in a club
- Participate in community center events
- Do volunteer work
- Spend more time with family and friends
- Get involved in political action
- Get involved in youth activities—Big Brothers, Big Sisters, scouts
- _____
- _____
- _____

Entertainment

- Watch TV and movies
- Play card and board games
- Travel
- Do crosswords, acrostics, math games
- Dine out
- Go to concerts, plays
- Go to ball games and other athletic events
- Go to an amusement park, a circus, a theme park
- Go miniature golfing
- _____
- _____
- _____

3. Contradict Permission-giving Thoughts

On the form below, write down your high-risk situations and the permission-giving thoughts or rationalizations you typically come up with. Then compose "permission-denying" thoughts to counteract them. Permission-denying thoughts should be rational counter arguments—logical, reasonable things you can say to yourself to dismantle your rationalizations.

Craving Situation	Permission-giving Thought	Permission-denying Thought
_____	_____	_____
_____	_____	_____
_____	_____	_____
_____	_____	_____
_____	_____	_____
_____	_____	_____
_____	_____	_____
_____	_____	_____
_____	_____	_____

Here are some examples:

Craving Situation	Permission-giving Thought	Permission-denying Thought
Guys say, let's go to bar after work	I can handle it. Don't be a wet blanket.	This is one of the situations I've decided to avoid. Don't risk it.
George orders wine with dinner	One glass won't hurt.	One glass is one too many. Turn that wine glass upside down.
Watching TV, want a joint	I'm all alone, nobody needs to know.	I'll know. One puff and it's six months of being clean down the drain.
Christmas party, want to put rum in my eggnog	I'm nervous as a cat. This will loosen me up, make me more social.	Nervous is better than drunk. Go tell someone how nervous you are.

It's a good idea to write your best rational reasons for not drinking or drugging on a small file card, and to carry it with you in your purse or wallet.

4. Cope With Cravings

In this step you will identify what happens just before you have a permission-giving thought, in the split-second before you realize that you'd like to take a drink or do drugs. This will help you focus on the feelings and thoughts that come up for you in everyday stressful situations.

To review the sequence outlined earlier in the chapter, this is how relapse progresses: Something happens, you have beliefs and thoughts that interpret the situation, you feel bad, and a craving for drugs or alcohol arises. This step, coping with cravings, attacks the sequence at the feelings and thoughts stage.

Make copies of the form below, and carry one around with you all the time. As soon as possible after you get a craving for drugs or alcohol, write down the situation, what you were feeling, and whatever thoughts were in your head. Continue to record situations until you have covered most of the high-risk situations you described in the previous section.

Situation	Feelings	Thoughts	Coping Thoughts
_____	_____	_____	_____
_____	_____	_____	_____
_____	_____	_____	_____
_____	_____	_____	_____
_____	_____	_____	_____
_____	_____	_____	_____
_____	_____	_____	_____
_____	_____	_____	_____
_____	_____	_____	_____
_____	_____	_____	_____
_____	_____	_____	_____
_____	_____	_____	_____
_____	_____	_____	_____

Situation. Remember that the situation doesn't have to be an external event. It may be no more elaborate than a certain mood you get into, just sitting, doing nothing, thinking about your past or future.

Feelings. After identifying the situation, briefly describe your feelings—bored, anxious, scared, angry, or whatever. The feeling is usually the easiest thing to identify in this exercise (and will usually be a negative feeling).

Thoughts. Underneath your feeling, actually occurring just before it, there will always be some thoughts. Write down whatever you were thinking. The ideas may or may not seem to relate to the feeling that followed. That doesn't matter. If you can't identify any thoughts, try running the situation over in your mind like a movie in slow motion. Imagine that your thoughts are like a narrator who's explaining the plot of the movie just for your benefit. Being able to identify individual thoughts—to "catch yourself in the act" of thinking something—becomes easier with time and practice.

Coping Thoughts. Compose a coping thought that dismantles the thought occurring just before the feeling. The coping thought is your logical comeback to a bad feeling that can send you into a tailspin.

Here is an example of a form filled out by Sylvia over a one-week period.

Situation	Feelings	Thoughts	Coping Thoughts
Dog pees on rug	Exasperated	He's doing it on purpose	He's only a pup—don't take it personally.
Son refuses to go to school	Furious	He's rebelling—I have no power over him	Calm down—I can figure this out
Have to drive on freeway	Anxious	I'll get us both killed	I've done this before—just keep breathing
Watching TV show about famines	Sad, hopeless	So much pain in the world, kids are so vulnerable	I'm doing my best, I'm a good mother
Reading a love story	Sad	Wish I had a man in my life	I just got divorced—these things take time
George says let's go out	Pleased, but nervous	He has to like me	Don't obsess—take him at face value

5. Change Core Beliefs and Automatic Thoughts

This is in-depth work that will take longer, but can yield more profound and far-reaching results. In this exercise, you delve below the surface of negative thoughts to find the deeply-ingrained core beliefs that you hold to be true about yourself, the world, and other people.

Make copies of the form on the next page and carry one around with you.

Situation	Feelings	First Thoughts	Second Thoughts

The first two columns will be familiar from the previous exercise. Only the "first thought" and "second thought" columns are new.

First Thought. As we said before, underneath the feeling (actually occurring in between the situation and the feeling) there will always be some thoughts. They may be hard to figure out, since they are often quiet and quick. The first thought is likely to be an automatic, habitual thing you say to yourself which typically makes you feel anxious or scared or mad or bad in some other way.

In this column, don't list craving thoughts like, "I'd like a drink," or permission-giving thoughts, like, "It will help me sleep." Keep looking for thoughts that occur earlier, and are more closely related to making you feel bad.

Second Thought. This is the hardest thought to observe, since it comes from a deeper level. What you're after here is a core belief, something you believe in your guts to be true about your ability, your safety, your worth, your power, your freedom, or your expectations of love and justice from others. The beliefs underlying your bad feelings may not have an obvious, logical connection to the situation at hand.

Don't worry if you have trouble with this part of the exercise. The cycle from situation to belief to thought to feeling to craving happens very quickly. Not only does each cycle happen quickly, but one cycle leads to another in an intertwining pattern of events, thoughts, and feelings that can be very hard to dissect. It takes a lot of practice before you can focus on one separate craving cycle and backtrack all the way to core beliefs.

Try imagining the situation in super slow motion, like a movie shown one frame at a time. Try to hear your thoughts as a voice-over narration of the slow-motion film.

Here is Sylvia's form, using the same situations as in the previous exercise, but trying to delve a little deeper into her thinking:

Situation	Feeling	First Thought	Second Thought
Dog pees on rug	*Exasperated*	*He's doing it on purpose*	*Everyone's out to get me*
Son refuses to go to school!	*Furious*	*He's rebellious just like his Dad*	*Nothing I do seems to work, I have no control in my life*
Have to drive on freeway to take Mom to doctor	*Anxious*	*I'll get us both killed*	*The world's full of danger*
Watching TV show about famines	*Sad, hopeless*	*So much pain in the world, kids are so vulnerable*	*Everything's hopeless, we're all doomed*
Reading a love story	*Sad*	*Wish I had a man in my life*	*Nobody loves me*

| *George says let's go out* | *Pleased but nervous* | *He has to like me* | *He just feels sorry for me—things never work out* |

Sylvia began to see that certain themes lay under her anxiety and anger. At her core, she believed that she just wasn't lovable, and that the world was a dangerous place where she had to keep her guard up. Considering the violent and unstable family she grew up in, these were understandable beliefs. But they were getting in the way of her happiness and her recovery from chemical dependence.

Compose Alternative Core Beliefs

When you have identified the beliefs that underlie your negative thinking, you can make up affirmations that contradict those beliefs. Practice saying your affirmations to yourself when you feel bad and the old cravings start to come over you.

These are the new core beliefs that Sylvia composed to counteract her old ones:

I am a lovable person.
I deserve to live well and be happy.
I can love and be loved.
I can make changes for the better.
I can make a safe world for myself and my child.

Another way to explore core beliefs, and start changing them, is to do more advanced addiction recovery work involving your inner child, co-dependence, and characteristics of adult children of alcoholics. Those areas are beyond the scope of this book. If this kind of exploration interests and excites you, check out the recovery section of a good bookstore.

Putting It All Together in Imagery

Pick the most dangerous high-risk situation you can't avoid. Pick one that is actually coming up, or likely to come up for you in the near future.

Lie down where you won't be disturbed. Get comfortable and do some deep breathing. Scan your body for tension, and relax all your muscles. See the chapter on relaxation if you have trouble getting relaxed.

Visualize the situation you have chosen. Take some time to make it seem real: add all the sights, the sounds, even the smells and tactile sensations that you will actually experience.

See yourself entering the situation. Imagine having all the temptations, the automatic thoughts, the cravings, the permission-giving thoughts, and so on. See yourself almost taking action, then successfully not drinking or drugging.

When Doug, a police detective in a big city, tried this exercise, he imagined meeting his partner and colleagues in a local police bar to discuss cases and unwind. This was a high-risk situation that he couldn't always avoid. He visualized coming into the cool dim bar after a long hot day on the streets. He smelled the smoky, beery atmosphere, heard the rumble of voices, and the clink of bottles and glasses.

He felt himself sliding into the familiar vinyl booth seat, saying "Hi" to his partner and a couple of other cops on their team. He let the familiar thought run through his mind: "This is where I belong, it's safe here, I can relax." He imagined these automatic thoughts bringing up the usual craving: "I'd like a beer," and the usual permission-giving thoughts: "I deserve it after a day like today. Just a quick cold one to take the edge off."

Then Doug imagined himself using some of his permission-denying thoughts: "It always starts with just one, but it never stops there. Coke is just as cold, and I can stay in control."

He visualized signaling the waitress, having her come over, and heard himself actually start to order a beer, then change his mind: "I'll have a draft . . . no, make that a coke."

Special Considerations: When You Do Lapse

Every lapse is not a relapse. Just because you slip and take a drink or do one line of cocaine, or take a couple of hits of grass, it doesn't mean you have to have a full-blown relapse.

Your relapse plan should include a firm resolution that if you do slip and take a drink or do drugs, you will climb right back on the wagon again, not slide all the way to the bottom before you bounce back. Take a moment right now to write out your relapse plan:

I, _____, plan never to drink or do drugs again.
If I do slip, for whatever reason, under whatever circumstances, I plan to quit
immediately. When I slip or feel myself about to lapse back into my old ways,
I will call _____. I will go _____,
and I will do _____.

Include whom you will call, what meeting or group or person you will go to, and what action you will take, such as leaving a party right away, asking to be driven home, and so on.

A Final Word

Congratulations on all the work you have done in this book. It has taken courage, patience, and determination to get this far. At this point you have probably achieved a year or more of abstinence. Maybe you had lapses on the way. Maybe it took you two years to rack up twelve months of sobriety. So be it.

In recovering from addiction, there is really no final word, unless it's an epitaph. Each day is another opportunity to choose between alcohol and drugs or living a straight and sober life. It does get easier, but it never gets simple. That's because quitting alcohol and drugs means choosing to live your life as a full-scale, full-time adult human being. And that's not a simple task for anyone.

Pat yourself on the back, and take credit for every inch of progress you've made. Forgive yourself for the mistakes and detours along the way. Know that there is more adventure ahead, and that you can enjoy it as a sober, free person.

Bibliography

Alcoholism and Drug Research Communications Center. *SCI-MAT: Science Matters in the Battle Against Alcoholism and Related Diseases* (Newsletter).

Anonymous. 1976. *Alcoholics Anonymous: The Story of How Many Thousands of Men and Women Have Recovered from Alcoholism*. Third edition. New York: Alcoholics Anonymous World Services, Inc.

Anonymous. 1987. *The Twelve Steps, A Way Out*. San Diego, California: Recovery Publications.

Beck, Aaron T., Fred D. Wright, Cory F. Newman, Bruce S. Liese. 1993. *Cognitive Therapy of Substance Abuse*. New York: The Guilford Press.

Dorsman, Jerry. 1991. *How to Quit Drinking Without AA*. Newark, Delaware: New Dawn Publishing.

Erickson, Carlton K. and John T. O'Neill. 1995. "It is time." *Amythist, Newsletter of the National Council on Alcoholism and Drug Dependence*. Summer, Vol. 3, No. 2. pp1–2.

Erickson, Carlton K. and John T. O'Neill. 1995. "What Happened to TIQ Studies?" *Professional Counselor*. June p17.

Johnson, Vernon E. 1973. *I'll Quit Tomorrow*. New York: Harper & Row.

National Council on Alcoholism and Drug Dependence. *Amethyst* (Newsletter).

National Institute on Alcohol Abuse and Alcoholism. *Alcohol Alert* (Newsletter).

O'Keefe, Pip. 1980. *Sober Living Workbook*. Center City, Minnesota: Hazelden.

O'Neill, John T. 1996. "Voice of the victims—the key to consensus and support for alcoholism research." *Alcohol and Alcoholism*. Vol 30, No. 0.

O'Neill, John T. and Pat O'Neill. 1993. *Concerned Intervention: When Your Loved One Won't Quit Alcohol or Drugs.* Oakland, California: New Harbinger Publications.

O'Neill, John T. and Pat O'Neill. 1989. *Help to Get Help: When Someone Else's Drinking or Drugging Is Hurting You.* Austin, Texas: Creative Assistance Press.

Peniston, Eugene G., and Paul J. Kulkosky. "Alcoholic Personality and Alpha-Theta Brainwave Training." *Medical Psychotherapy,* 1990, Vol. 3, pp37–55.

Waisberg, Jodie L., and James E. Porter. 1994. "Purpose in life and outcome of treatment for alcohol dependence." *British Journal of Clinical Psychology.* Feb. Vol 33(1) pp49–63.